JOE FRANCIS

AN AMERICAN ENTREPRENUER

EDWIN KLEIN

ISBN Number 978-1-57087-739-1

Library of Congress Control Number 2008932126

Manufactured in the United States of America
01 02 03 04 05 10 9 8 7 6 5 4 3 2 1

Joseph Francis, Founder of The Barbers, 1933-1994

"Life has been a real adventure for me. I never dreamed from my humble beginnings that I, a person who came into this world with very little, without the advantage of a father's guidance or proper education both in knowledge and in culture, could or would rise to the level that I have.

People think that I was driven by the money, or the fame, or the prestige. None of that was important to me. Yes, it was nice, but to be able to accomplish what I set out to do was reward enough. The famous artist leaves his or her canvas, the sculptor leaves their carving, we leave our children and their children's children—that is our greatest legacy to the world."

INTRODUCTION

In writing this book, I gathered stories and opinions from many of the friends and business associates of this charismatic, engaging and sometimes enigmatic business leader, whose mind and body seemed to be always in perpetual motion.

Joe Francis had an innate ability to attract the best people while leading by example and capitalizing on the "laws of attraction." His powerful self-confidence, positive outlook, faith in his associates, perseverance and tenacity took him to the top of what had been considered a mundane industry. Joe's vision and his grasp of the actions necessary to transform the barber industry took root in a tiny one-chair barbershop in West St. Paul, Minnesota in 1957. Joe Francis was harboring a dream in his heart, a dream to be the best in his field and do whatever it took to get there!

Joe's persona had attracted to him the most meaningful relationship of his life...his girlfriend, stalwart wife, partner and driving force, Florence (Marquardt)

Francis, who survived Joe to become the Chairman of the Board of Directors of Joe's company, "The Barbers, Inc." The Barbers and its brands: Cost Cutters, We Care Hair, and City Looks International, sold their franchise organization to Regis Hair Salons in 1999 while Florence (Flo) Francis was the Chair. This isn't just a biography of a man in the "hair" industry; it's a story about the triumph of overcoming a struggle with poverty, challenges and grief. It's a story about unending optimism and determination. It's about the "American Dream" in its finest form!

Edwin Klein

DEDICATION

Within this book beats a heart. Just as no birth can be sustained without its lifeblood, so too, no organization can survive without a pulse. The Barbers franchise concept was born when a diverse group of people imbued the organization with faith, hope and an abundance of hard work to bring it to "lift off." Joe Francis provided the launch pad; they provided the fuel and I was in the thick of it all the way with my loving, kind and courageous husband, Joe. This book is dedicated to Joey, Susan, Barbara, Jeanne and John, our children, who made the journey with us.

Mrs. Florence Francis

PREFACE

Global business leaders have a different clock, a different tempo, a different way of seeing ahead and removing cultural, social and political barriers. In 1992, after the fall of Communism in Russia, Joe Francis opened the first "western concept" Hair Styling Salon and Spa in the heart of Moscow.

Who could have guessed a Lebanese kid born into poverty and family struggle, a kid who dropped out of high school, would create a company, develop it and move it to the top in it's industry, take it public and then take it to Russia?

> *Life has been a real adventure for me. I never dreamed from my humble beginnings that I, a person who came into this world with very little, without the advantage of a father's guidance or a proper education in either culture or knowledge, would rise to the level I have.*
>
> Joe Francis

In 1963, we risked it all, signed a lease for space that required us to pay more rent per month than we had ever dreamed of making. We signed for a loan, put up all our furniture and car for the collateral. Fortunately, the bank didn't know the furniture was from the Salvation Army and the car was a $50.00 'Junker'. We opened on a shoestring!

Mrs. Florence Francis

When Joe went, it was like Superman died. I don't know how to tell you what I felt. I'll always miss him.

Ron Battern
(Salon Owner)/Franchisee

Loyalty? There was nothing any of us wouldn't have done for the company or Joe. He always called us family and we always looked to him for guidance.

Marv Alvheim
(Salon Owner)/Franchisee

I got a piece of the man…a piece of the dream…a piece of the ride. What more could you ask?

Earl Faulkner
(Salon Owner)/Franchisee

It was Christmas away from my native Sweden, not many friends…you can imagine. Joe called to say 'if you're not too busy, come by and spend Christmas with us'. Joe and Flo knew I was alone…do you know how warm that made me feel?

Bertil Anderberg
(Salon Owner)/Franchisee

CONTENTS

A TRIBUTE

PACKED HOUSE

Jeff Roberts, a prominent hair salon owner, had profound respect for Joe—even though they had often had their differences—and Joe had the same kind of respect for Jeff. In 1993, by talking with many of Joe's business associates, franchisees, management staff and friends, Jeff was inspired to put a recognition event together for Joe. He knew Joe was not going to make it—that the cancer was taking its toll. Jeff was concerned that many people would regret not having an opportunity to tell Joe how much he meant to them, if Joe were to pass unexpectedly. He talked to Flo about it and Flo hosted a *meeting* at the Francis home so they could discuss this idea.

Jeff tried to be as tactful and subtle as he could but here's what he said: "Joe, from what I'm hearing, you're pretty sick and you're not going to get better. If that's true, even though we've been at odds many times through the years, I've gotta tell ya—I'm one of your biggest admirers. Joe, it dawns on me that if I want to express that to you, many others might want to be able to do the same thing and they might not want to wait until it's too late. So, I'm telling you right now, I want to put a dinner event together to recognize you and there are a lot of people who want to help me."

Well, Joe showed his meek and humble self. He said, "Naw, nobody would come to that." But he knew if I said it was going to happen, it would. I knew Joe would treasure this—I had to get it done! Well, they finally agreed. So with Joe and Flo, mostly with Flo, we started putting it together. I wanted their friends involved too; not just the business people I knew.

It turned out to be a big event! We had it at the Radisson Hotel in St. Paul and the twin cities media covered it. More than 450 people attended the black-tie-optional event. It was packed! We had the Irv Williams group for the band, flowers, great dinner—it was a huge success. Joe had asked me to be the MC but I knew I'd be too emotional. Joe just meant so much to me. So, we got Michael Cole, who'd been with Joe as a Director of Training. He couldn't have been better. I did agree to be the keynote speaker but I could hardly make it through the introduction. There wasn't a dry eye in the house. Rocco Altobelli, a well known salon entreprenuer, also spoke—it was big, really big for Joe. It took me about five months to pull this all together. It wasn't maudlin though, it was upbeat.

You know, as much as Joe looked forward to it, he was actually nervous. He stayed in a suite at the Radisson that evening and he was interviewed by the media that afternoon. It wasn't normal for Joe to be nervous but he seemed to be. I think he was overwhelmed, you know—Joe was so humble. He couldn't believe that so many people wanted to be there. I had a great committee for this; they really did all they could to help. I'll tell you; this was a spiritual thing for me—to do this for my friend Joe.

It was one of the highest points of my life. I saw him as a bootstrap guy that was able to come back again and again and again! He just kept comin'! I saw Joe as an unsung hero. He was often in a lonely place. He was criticized—people out for his hide—that kind of thing but he was a decent man and always rose above it. Some people didn't see the nobleness of Joe's character but I did. I think the event we held for him prepared him for more serenity—a serenity he didn't know he had within him. By the time he passed, he seemed to be a very peaceful man. I think he passed with a real sense of fulfillment and achievement, not just as a businessman, but as a human being too.

CHAPTER 1

A SEED IN MAZEPPA, 1933

What makes a man? What is it that builds his character? In the case of Joe Francis, he came from good stock. His mother, Sadie George, began her epic voyage to America from Beirut, Lebanon in 1928 on a two-story freighter. She traveled with her brother, Said. She was 16, a 5′3″ dynamo with black hair, brown eyes and a fair complexion. Her parents, Joseph and Mary George had immigrated to America 15 years earlier and left Sadie and Said in the custody of grandparents and other relatives. What little money her parents could scrape together to send back for their children, would fall through the cracks. The parents later learned that the money was spent on other family needs and not on Sadie and Said. Needless to say, the children had a difficult childhood.

When Sadie and Said arrived at Ellis Island, they were shocked to learn that they would have to pass an

Entrance test. No one had prepared them for this! This wasn't a problem for Said. He could speak fluent Arabic (their native language) and French. He could also read and write and the test was offered in Arabic. Sadie, unfortunately, was not educated. There was no way Sadie could pass this test. They were gripped with fear; they had no money and returning to Lebanon was not an option. Said would not abandon her and he wouldn't accept turning back. His determination and creative juices kicked in as he relentlessly badgered the officials until he convinced them and they finally gave in and allowed them both entry into the United States.

Their parents and siblings were living in McIntosh, South Dakota, so Said and Sadie boarded a train and headed west. When they were settled, since they did not have the skills they would need to be independent in America, it was time for school and learning. Because of their lack of English language skills, they were placed in the 1st Grade. The humiliation of being teenagers in classes with much-younger classmates was unbearable and they quit school soon after enrolling.

For the next few years, Sadie was relegated to household chores, as was the custom in her native country. There were more surprises and tests to come her way soon. In Lebanon, marriages were arranged by the family when a girl reached marriageable age and so her parents betrothed Sadie to be married to a countryman, Joseph Peter Francis. Although Sadie was concerned that Joseph was twenty-five years older than her, they were married in 1932. Within a year, they moved to a small farm he had bought in Mazeppa, Minnesota. She never really made an emotional recovery from the marriage arrangement but survivor that she was, she endured and stayed the course until Joseph's death thirteen years later.

Joe Francis was born into this setting on December 1, 1933, the oldest of four children, in a small farmhouse without the benefit of running water, indoor plumbing or electricity—his childhood could well have been called harsh. The old farmhouse was not well built and seemed to breathe with the wind at night. Far too often, the family was nearly penniless. He later recounted going to the icebox on several occasions when hungry, only to find it empty. What little they had, would have to stretch a long way.

Joe was born with adventure in his heart, and he loved challenges. Once, as a boy, when Joe's dad was helping a neighbor during the threshing season, a cow somehow got out of his dad's fenced pasture. His father told Joe to try to find the cow; he was afraid it might get into the nearby Zumbrota River. Joe, with his cousin Bill tagging along, found the cow. Sure enough, it was in the river. Joe couldn't swim but he did know how to hold his breath and bob up and down from the river bottom. Cousin Bill objected—telling Joe, "That's crazy, are you nuts? You could drown." But Joe was determined and he jumped in, bobbed out to the cow and brought her back. This was good practice for Joe, as he'd be bobbing for air and taking even more daring risks in his future business career!

Joe's childhood certainly wasn't all play and no work. This young man was often up before daybreak to haul pails of milk to the neighbor's farm; pretty ominous trip for a lad of ten or eleven when many times there was not even the benefit of starlight or the moon.

Perhaps the seed of his work ethic was planted while toiling in the fields behind his Dad and the horse-drawn plow. Or, it might have come from observing his Mom fetch wood for the stove, pump water at the outside well for cooking or for washing clothes and hauling it into the house. She also had to bake and prepare meals for the family, sew and mend their clothes and see that the children got their schoolwork done. Schooling, for a woman who never had much of a chance to learn, became a problem between Sadie, and her husband Joseph.

Joe's dad was known to be the hardest-working man around. He felt the farm should come before anything else and he expected the whole family to help. However, he was barely able to eke out even a meager living. He had very little equipment, spoke poor English, the ground was hard, lacked nutrients and crops were poor. The family suffered immensely.

In Mazeppa, the children got to their one room school by horse-drawn cart. The school was miles away and had only one teacher who taught all eight grades. Since this was in the Minnesota "snow belt," their winter ride was by horse-drawn sleigh. Hot bricks for their feet and blankets to cover them were their only comfort.

One day, there was a particularly bad snow storm and while Sadie was bundling the children for school, she noticed that little Joe's shoes had worn so thin they were useless. Without hesitation, she removed her shoes and had him try them on. Not the best fit but at least his feet were protected. Off he went in his Mom's shoes. Because the family lived hand-to-mouth, clothing often had to be shared too. Severe weather and bitter winters would take their toll and the children often missed school as a result.

No doubt, Sadie's childhood flashed back into her mind. Perhaps she relived the fear she felt when she landed in America; and the disaster that could have happened because she didn't have any education. In any case, Sadie wouldn't have it—her children were going to be educated no matter what.

This schooling issue led to a rift between Sadie and her husband Joseph. Both stood firm in their convictions and, in a very unpopular move for those times, Sadie left Mazeppa. She took the children and moved to a St. Paul neighborhood close to better schools. Times were tough, clothing was minimal, food was scarce and there were no frills. Sadie worked very hard to make ends meet, plucking chickens at a Dahlgren's Produce and as a maid at The St. Paul Hotel. Joe's dad couldn't get by with just farming so he took a job with Kopper's Coke, a coal plant in St. Paul, MN. He also continued to work the farm from spring through fall.

Young Joe loved going back to work the farm with his Dad during the growing seasons. He'd take the bus from St. Paul to Mazeppa, and then walk eight to ten miles to the farm. Tough as his Dad could be on him, Joe never complained about his adult-sized chores. His father taught him how to cook and take care of the home. Joe always remembered and loved this private time and lengthy conversations with his dad.

Eventually, Joseph must have realized he was fighting a losing battle and he auctioned off many of the family belongings and used the money to buy a small hobby farm right on the outskirts of St. Paul, close to schools. Sadie relented and the family was reunited on the new farm. The year was 1942. Joseph, died from a stroke just three years later. Joseph's death moved Joe, now just 12 years old, to position of head of the family. He remembered his mom coming to him and saying "you're the man of the house now." The struggle and toil continued. Sadie was forced to sell the Mazeppa farm for a pittance, and moved the family to the west side of St. Paul, across the street from her brother Said.

As you might expect, his father's death had a deep emotional effect on young Joe, one that surfaced again 38 years later. During a discussion with his family, Joe inadvertently said "When I was twelve, I died." Indeed, one might guess that what he meant to say was that when he was twelve years old his dad died. However, Joe's childhood died with his father and perhaps his subconscious was speaking the truth. His dad's work ethic lived on in Joe. And, thanks to the chores his dad had harnessed him with back on the farm, Joe could cook and manage household tasks. He took right over with his siblings as his Mom worked outside their home.

While she worked her jobs, Joe was also beginning his business career. His Uncle, Said George, ran a shoe repair business on South Robert St. in St. Paul. Said had learned the business from his father, who was a custom boot maker in South Dakota and earlier, back in Lebanon. It occurred to Joe that if he could have a few square feet in the corner of that shop, he could offer shoeshines. His uncle set him up with the goods and Joe was now shining shoes. He charged 15 cents a shine. His clientele at the shoe repair shop included a lot of men who worked in the nearby stockyards. They would come in with mud and manure on their boots and his uncle would escort them to the back door to scrape and clean them off before they got a shine.

Uncle Said was a blessing for Joe and a solid role model for his little nephew. They talked about customer service, business in general and the future. More than once, Said would tell Joe, "you see all this expensive equipment? You don't want to be in the shoe business." Pointing, he said, "look at the barber down the street...all he has to buy is a clipper, comb and scissors and he's in business—think about it!" When it came to business ideas, Joe was wide-awake and Said's advice began to take hold.

His tenure as a shoeshine boy and dealing with everyone from stockyard hands to bankers and attorneys helped Joe focus on his future. The "wheels" were always in motion with Joe and as an adjunct business to his growing shoe shine stand, he started delivering telegrams with his bicycle and also got a paper route. All this customer contact would pay off for him later. Every dime he made, he turned over to his mother for the household. He didn't know it but she put a lot of this money away for his future. Joe adored his mother, and with his own small savings from his paper route, he bought her a special wall mirror, a mirror that's still in the family.

As he grew into his teens, his experiences made him very savvy and he became quite "glib" as well. In dealing with a wide variety of customers and situations, he started developing impressive communication and business skills that led to many 'regulars'. He always had a great sense of humor, a quality that impressed a certain sweet young lady whom he would pursue with his heart and soul.

Florence Marquardt had been working for two years at her family's bakery, next door to George's shoe repair shop. The "guys" in neighborhood made it a point to stop at the bakery and chat, trying to get to know this cute 14 year old girl who was so bubbly and friendly. At the bakery, Florence did it all—prep work for baking, slicing and wrapping bread, taking phone orders and covering the sales counter. She often worked next to her dad, Bill Marquardt. He had a great sense of humor and would often toss a small ball of dough at Flo when she came to work after school. (Flo, of course, would toss it right back at her dad.)

One snowy winter day, as she walked from school to the bakery, she noticed something strange. This teenaged boy was going in and out of the shoe shop just cracking up, laughing and waving his arms around. As she got closer, she could see what he was up to. He had partially buried a wallet in the snow with a string attached to it. He would hide around the corner in the window of the shop and whenever a passerby would spot the wallet and stoop to pick it up, the boy would yank the string and pull it out of reach. "I couldn't help but watch him do this several times," Flo would later say, "he was having so much fun."

The teenage boy was Joe Francis and when he saw Flo watching him, he gave her a wink. Flo said she felt like flying, "he was so handsome, black curly hair and...what a smile!" Later the same day, just before closing time, as Joe shoveled the sidewalk in front of the shoe shop, he saw Flo locking up the bakery. He hustled over to her— "I'll shovel your walk for a free crispy." Flo was totally smitten! She gave him a bag of pastries and discovered in conversation that they both went to the same high school. The next day and everyday thereafter, Joe would meet Flo outside her freshman home room. But it was the day Joe jumped over the bakery counter and kissed her that Flo says she saw stars! This would be the start of a lifelong love affair. While Flo was always very aware of her own personal appearance, it didn't bother her that Joe would wear the same clothes to school almost every day—jeans, work boots, his leather flight jacket and a sailor's beanie cap when it was cold. He didn't have much but his character ran deep.

Flo was Lutheran and Joe was Catholic. This was not a romance her parents were ready to endorse. However, once they met Joe and noticed his kind manners and engaging personality, all was well. The courtship continued. Flo had the utmost respect for her parents. Her dad worked hard, was a model family man who was kind and good to his wife and children. Her mom, Edith, was a very talented lady and wonderful homemaker. She was a "jolly" soul who loved to entertain! Flo credits her social talents to her mother.

Flo graduated from St. Paul's Humboldt High School when she was sixteen and went to work for the Welfare Services at the State Capitol. She was always very frugal; she knew how to find a bargain, and even sewed her own clothes. Flo also had literary and acting talents. At the time, her wages were $262 dollars per month and she saved $200 each month! (She was already planning for her future wedding to Joe.)

On the other hand, Joe Francis, in a hurry to get on with his plans for the future, dropped out of high school his Junior year. There were more important—more exciting things to do than attend high school. The Navy seemed like a good idea to him but his plan to join was redirected when he found he needed a high school diploma or a trade. Harkening back to Uncle Said's advice, he decided to go to Barber school. Fortunately, he'd been hustling customers at the Barber school for shoe shines for a couple of years and with what he saved and the money his mother had put away for him, he had enough for his tuition. He learned to cut hair and would cut from 7:00 a.m. to 6:00 p.m. six days a week—then wash dishes at night in a nearby restaurant. When he'd get a short break to eat, he'd always give Flo a call. The two were inseparable. Joe was on a mission. Although he'd dropped out of high school, he graduated from Barber School as the youngest graduate ever in the state of Minnesota, at age seventeen!

His successful completion of the Barber School was quite an achievement. Joe was always ambitious, yet Flo understood the value of a high school diploma and urged him to go back to finish. He finally agreed and they graduated the same year, 1953, when she was sixteen and he was nineteen. So, in reality, Joe didn't "quit" high school...he just postponed his graduation.

Shortly after graduation in 1953, Joe was drafted into the Army and was stationed in Fort Carson, Colorado. Over the next 18 months, Flo continued to work hard and save most of what she made. In 1955, having saved enough money, they were married at Holy Family Church in St. Paul, Minnesota. Because Flo was Lutheran and Joe a Catholic, she agreed to satisfy the requirement of Joe's faith that any children would be raised as Catholic. After the wedding, they moved to Fort Carson, Colorado and into a tiny two-room apartment.

While Joe continued soldiering, Flo took a job at Colorado Springs City Hall. She was their receptionist and switchboard operator. Part of her duties included taking notes at the Planning Commission meetings, setting up press releases and reporting to various media. She caught on quickly and this experience would prove to be very valuable in the not-too-distant future.

A honeymoon ensued when Joe got a 30-day medical leave, after a hernia surgery, and the newlyweds headed for what would become a 2,300-mile trip through Mexico. Flo had also saved enough money to buy a new, $2,400 car, a Ford Fairlane. As they set out on their trip, they experienced some very bad weather but that didn't deter them. Sand storms, snowstorm in the mountains, little towns without streetlights, no one who spoke English, no problem, they were adventurous! On they went and the fun continued. During a storm on a pitch black night, they were inching along a crooked road and could only see a few feet past the headlights. For some reason, they decided to stop. They got out and walked a short distance in front of their car to assess the situation. There, a few feet away, was a wash out and a two hundred foot drop into a ravine. The newlyweds noticed several other couples (none of them American), who had tried to circumvent the washout by driving down the hill to the other side; there were some horses, junker cars and a bus, all slipping in the mud and wet grass. They followed suit, as Joe thought he could make it down the ravine and back up the other side. But within a few minutes, they were stuck like all the others. Mustering all their effort and leading a cooperative scheme that took all night, they all helped to push one car after another out of the dilemma until everyone was on their way again.

Eventually, they did make it to Mexico City, but by then their cash was depleted and it was time to head back. They only had enough money to buy gas. On the trip back to the base, Joe pushed it hard. He knew when he got back he could cut hair at the military PX and tide them over until payday. Joe always seemed to find the silver lining in any cloud that followed him. There was never a dull moment for the newlywed sweethearts. They often escaped their tiny two-room apartment to play tennis, with racquets Flo bought at the Salvation Army, or go camping in the nearby mountains.

Returning to St. Paul in December 1955, after Joe's Army discharge, he went to work as an apprentice Barber at Isaacs Barber Shop, essentially the same shop his Uncle Said used to point at to make an example. During his tenure there, he became more and more proficient at giving customer's their "best ever" flat top cuts. Flat tops were all the rage at the time and Joe would go on to win many competitions in the barbering world for his perfect cuts.

Joe's barbering career was launched, but he told Flo he felt totally "out of sync" and wondered if he should consider a different career. Flo did some research and found that the University of Minnesota offered a testing program for directing students to a career choice. She managed to get Joe into it and he was told he'd do well in the field of Criminology, possibly as a Private Investigator. Flo then discovered that the University of

Michigan offered the courses recommended and set up an interview for Joe. They were considering that he'd go there to get his degree in that field.

Soon after, they piled into their car with their three-week old first born son, Joey, and off they went to Michigan—baby bottles, formula, diapers and all. When they arrived, Joe found out during his interview that if he did a seven-year stint and got his Masters degree, he'd probably be earning only what he was now making as a Barber. He knew this wasn't the direction for him and so they returned to Minnesota. There just had to be more, something more exciting and challenging—something where he could make big money. He went back to the drawing board.

He'd always had an interest in the Real Estate business and the climate in Phoenix. He talked with Flo about the possibility of moving there, getting licensed and selling real estate. They had also discussed a more daring move to Australia or New Zealand. Phoenix? Flo was game. She was willing to pack up and start a whole new life. Risky, but then risk was a part of who they were. A problem that stood in their way was finances. In order to make the move, they'd have to clean up their bills, which never seemed to go away or even diminish. So, the Phoenix plan was put on the back burner.

Tough as times were and thin as the family "kitty" would often be, fun was never far away. The Francis family loved to entertain. It all started with the refreshments being just chips and lemonade. It would escalate in later years to include a multitude of weekend picnics and parties.

By the time Joe had put in a couple years at Isaacs Barber Shop, he could see the answer to getting ahead was to own his own business. So, in 1957, Joe opened his one-chair Barber Shop. He located an abandoned, beat up shop that would steal his evenings and weekends to patch up, paint and clean. However, the rent was cheap at $65 a month. Service and pride of accomplishment was important to him. He wanted his customers to be happy and look forward to being waited on and pampered. With Joe, the customer was always "King." Barber shops back then provided a sort of "cultural cave" for men. Where else could you catch up on the local and national sports, politics, child rearing for teenagers and so much more? The Barber Shop at the time, was a trip to a "man's world" and if you were a kid waiting for a haircut, you'd come away with all the latest sports news to share with your sandlot buddies.

And talk about back up! Flo didn't need any direction. She put ads in the paper, made up flyers, wrote press releases, got Joe to join the Chamber of Commerce and other business clubs—and—with children in tow, she'd hit the street placing flyers on door knobs! Their daughter, Jeanne, reflects: "I think I was involved in putting out flyers almost from the time I could walk. My parents were so enthusiastic and we kids had so much fun helping. The spirit of my parents—their attitudes—I mean they were always so very positive."

It was also in 1957 that Joe would make his first of many real estate investments, a duplex. They rented out the top and lived downstairs. It would prove to be a wise move and influenced his propensity to search for more real estate.

Flo made every penny count during these lean years. She remembers finding a baptismal garment at the Salvation Army for 50 cents when she needed something for Joey's upcoming Baptism. Using her sewing skills, Flo was able to turn her 50-cent purchase into an outfit that any Mom would be proud of and no one was any the wiser.

Neighbors, George and Celia Lamb reflect—"Our street was torn up for repairs. It was pretty bad, dusty when dry, muddy and full of ruts when wet. We couldn't help but notice we had a new family on the block. The fellow looked familiar to both of us and always seemed to have this big smile on his face. And the lady—well, she was something else. We'd see her coming home in this Ford Fairlane, just barreling down the street. She had to gun it to make sure she didn't get stuck in the ruts and she handled that thing like a tank. She'd finally swing that car around, with her little boy in the back, and make it up the driveway. George would say 'my God, she did it again—how'd she do it?'"

So, Celia decided she just had to go meet this fascinating lady. As it turned out, Celia had gone to grade school with Joe. George remembered Flo from the family bakery and Joe as an altar boy at the church. They became lifelong friends from that time on. George would say that he was impressed with Joe's enthusiasm and penchant for learning. He was always reading and reaching for more.

When Joe went public with his company, says George, I bought in. I purchased a block of his initial stock. He'd tell me about his dream of building a big organization and Flo—she was so supportive—they were really a great team. Joe was always upbeat, I never heard him complain. If he had a problem, he'd just look for a solution. It never got the best of him. And Flo, she was always taking classes—stretching and trying to improve herself as well. They earned every penny they ever made."

The two families went on many vacations together and often partied at the Francis home on Lake Gervais in the later years. The Lamb's hung onto their stock in Joe's company until after his death. Joe seemed to appreciate that they never sold out. In fact, they often bought more when it took a dive, betting the company would bounce back.

After Joe passed, they sent a letter to Flo, telling her that because of the hard work she and Joe had put in through the years, they (the Lamb's) had enjoyed some wonderful trips around the world and back. They said their standard of living had improved as a result of owning that stock. Friends and relatives who invested with Joe and Flo were impressed with their sincerity and interest in others.

Within a year after opening his first shop, Joe, this fledgling entrepreneur, would expand to a two-man shop by hiring Roy Oakes to join him. Years later, Roy would say "Joe was the best boss. When he hired me he said 'That's your chair now Roy—run it like it's your own business. Do as you like and you'll build up a clientele and make it!' Joe was a good man all around and we became good buddies too." For a short time, the two-chair shop seemed rewarding but for Joe things were still moving in slow motion. He liked the fact that hair keeps growing and his customer kept coming back, but he always felt there should be more. He was always looking to raise the bar. He knew that the most successful businessmen had learned how to expand their careers through alignment with others. If he didn't learn how to put this in motion, he'd be a small operator until retirement and certainly wouldn't be able to provide his growing family with the life he wanted them to have.

What to do? It was a period of time to explore the horizon, to search his soul, make a decision, set some goals and focus on achievement. Joe would say, "I see the whole world going by and here I am with my clippers and comb and what am I doing? Where's it all going?" He was restless, and even though he was only 23 years old, he didn't want to be in a limited job.

After much discussion and thought, Joe and Flo decided that when they traveled to various Barber and Beauty shows, they'd check out what other salon operators were doing. Surely the industry wasn't as dead-end or mundane as it seemed. There was no Internet, no Google and no easy way to do due diligence. Trade journals didn't help either; it was hit-the-road time. And what they found was a desperate industry.

During a trip to NYC, they visited many salons. Most salon owners were wallowing in the same not-too-promising future and complacent at that. No guru's in sight, no one moving in a more positive direction. Joe and Flo felt like they were standing in 'no mans' land. Again, they wondered, what should we do? (Maybe they'd find the answer at the next show that was coming up soon in Chicago.)

Joe wasn't just about aspirations, goals, achievement and making more money in order to satisfy *himself*. If there was anyone in the world he wanted to impress, it was his sweetheart wife. He would endeavor to do that until his last breath.

There was a fuzzy dream in place but bills still had to be paid and the family fed. In an effort to support his future in the hair care industry, Joe became a part-time stockbroker, postal stamp vending machine owner and match-book advertising salesman. His backup teams for these endeavors included Flo and the kids putting stamps into small plastic bubbles. These would sell for 25 cents in the stamp vending machines. The accumulating quarters made a small but welcome addition to the family bank account. Joe and his little boy, Joey, would travel their vending route to fill the machines, pick up quarters, bring them back to Flo. She'd deposit them in the bank every week.

In addition, Joe talked Roy Oakes, his second-chair man in the barbershop, into being a partner in a popcorn truck operation that consisted of a used truck fitted with a popcorn maker. They'd get done cutting hair, pull the truck out of the garage and hit the streets. Ringing a bell, beeping a horn and calling out "hot popcorn," they cruised neighborhood streets.

These early enterprises never made a lot of money but they did make a contribution to the family's "get-by" lifestyle. Since the Francis family loved to entertain at their sparsely furnished home, this pocket change made a positive difference. Through the accumulation of coins and many single dollars, Flo was able to furnish their home with some used furniture and her home-made curtains and drapes. All his extra time-consuming, hardly rewarding activity kept the fire going in Joe's heart; this was not enough, he'd find some way to do better, provide more, and make his wife and family proud!

He knew he was on the way to something big and though many stood by in a skeptical posture, Joe was going to get it done!

CHAPTER 2

AGAINST ALL ODDS

One of the greatest assets I had was Flo. She believed in me, gave me strength and a lot of class. I owe her greatly for that.

Joe Francis

Slow motion and Joe Francis were not a mix. He found that his two-man shop didn't fan the flames in his heart either. It was never going to be enough but what direction should he take? For Joe, an earthshaking event was right around the corner.

While at a Barber/Beauty show in Chicago in '62, Joe and Flo met an English barber who was involved in using a new technique in Europe called the "razor cut." Joe was known as a flat top (crew cut) expert but as you might guess, he was becoming bored with the simplicity and day-to-day routine. He found this razor cut idea totally intriguing and it made his heart pump—finally, something new! The razor cut involved the use of a straight razor rather than traditional scissors and clippers. This was new and exciting and Joe immediately embraced the concept.

There were some major differences. The razor cut was a 30-45 minute process unlike a 6-8 minute flat top cut. The hair was cut wet and afterward styled with the aid of a blow dryer. The result was that the hair appeared very sleek, tapered, thicker and fuller, a huge departure from any standard cut. Joe, being fast on the uptake and always ambitious, was drawn to the possibilities. "Right then, I decided to become an expert in European razor cutting," he said. He hired the Englishman to come to his St. Paul shop and teach him and Roy Oakes, his second-chair man, how to do razor cuts. But there was a serious hurdle to overcome. This extended process would require a higher cost to the customer. Joe figured he'd have to get $5.75 per cut versus his present charge of $1.75. Would the customer think he was getting "clipped" or cut? This was 1962 and $5.75 for a haircut, even with styling, in the conservative, grass roots Minnesota market may be more than the customer would be willing to pay? Only time would tell.

Many barbers remember going to union meetings about this time, where it was proposed that haircut prices be raised by 25 cents. Bob Amon, a barber back then, (who eventually came to work with The Barbers) remembers those meetings. "When they talked about a 25 cent increase, everybody just about went into shock!

We thought everyone would start cutting hair at home and the customer wouldn't pay that extra quarter!"

Roy Oakes said: "I knew Joe had guts and I believed he was always ahead of the game, I went with it but I didn't stick with it." Many of their regulars didn't go for Joe's pitch to convert them either. A few did but most preferred the traditional cut and the lesser price. Most men would've stopped right there but not Joe, something about this felt right to him.

At a late night dinner table discussion in the Francis home, Flo said, "You know what Joe? I think what this business needs is some class, I mean *real* class! Sure, it will cost more to design and set up an upscale shop but it would be something new and exciting. You have such exceptional customer service skills, you're such a great barber and you've really caught on to the razor cut idea; you could do it Joe! You could start a whole new thing!"

Joe became inspired as he listened, he felt if anyone had class, it was Flo. He could see that with her help they could do it. A vision, although a little blurry, started to come into focus. They were *on* to something! Joe could feel the juices flowing, he really felt excited. But while he was envisioning all this, he realized he wasn't quite there yet, there was still more to learn.

Traveling to shows—from Chicago to California, he started learning all he could from any operator involved in this new cutting approach and Salon concept. Deep down, he was sure about his vision and passionate about becoming an expert in the razor cut arena. In Hollywood, he consulted with renowned celebrity hairstylist, Jay Sebring, who was a leader in the West Coast men's hairstyling movement. Sebring's (razor cut) clientele included many movie stars like Robert Wagner, James Garner and Cliff Robertson.

Back in St. Paul with a renewed and refreshed attitude, Joe's wheels were spinning at a high revolution. He was always proactive and about a year before this, he'd put something into practice that was not usual in the men's barbering industry, especially in the Midwest; setting *appointments* with his clients. It was a novel idea and made sense, good customer service sense. The customer didn't have to wait and it was a better business plan for Joe. Flo sent out press releases, announcing the appointment process and the benefit to the customer. She was always in the forefront when it came to getting Joe's business in the headlines.

Joe knew that in order to get the razor-cut concept off the ground, he needed to be in a more affluent neighborhood. He was determined to find the right location and bring his dream to fruition. The search began. Actually, Flo's *talent* would help Joe move forward with his dream.

Flo had auditioned for and won the lead in a play with a local theatre group. Joe and Roy had sold their popcorn venture and with Joe home in the evenings, Flo was able to pursue her personal interests in acting, something that Flo loved to do. Joe, drove her to rehearsals and often stayed to enjoy the shtick, humor and antics of the acting troupe.

One evening after he dropped Flo off for rehearsal, he slipped out of the theatre to take a walk. It was a damp, dark, bone-chilling night and as he walked along the main street in St. Paul's Highland Village, an affluent neighborhood, he passed a "For Rent" sign in a strip center. Peering through the window, he could see what had been a deli. There was a long lunch counter, stools, an empty showcase and the space was a little beat up. He thought back to the day he had found his present location. Should he do it all again? The dimensions might work for an upscale hairstyling shop. Joe was very excited and couldn't wait to tell his thespian wife about the new location. He rushed into the theatre, and announced his discovery to Flo. That's how Joe operated—decisions were quick and spontaneous.

But there was bad news, they needed to discuss the rent. Joe said "it's *only* $400 a month and we *only* need to sign an *eleven-year* lease." At that time, they were renting his two-man shop for $65 per month, and considering that $400 was more money than he was making, this would be a huge commitment. Flo recalls "I was so afraid, I cried—I thought we'd go bankrupt."

They had a successful business, were making good money, they owned their home (with a mortgage, of course), and were able to entertain friends and relatives. Considering $400 a month just for rent, were they going to risk it all on a "hope-they-come" dream? Flo respected and loved Joe, and though very concerned, she became enthusiastic about the challenge. "My contemporaries thought I was goofy," Joe would say 20 years later in an interview. This man was like a powerful cruise liner without a rudder. He had his location nailed; his dream was in place, but where was the money going to come from? No problem, Joe thought, he would just go to the bank.

He had demonstrated a total commitment to this endeavor, the side jobs, stamp vending, selling mutual funds and matchbooks, all had to go. This was going to be big, and Joe knew he could pull it off.

> *In 1963 we risked it all, signed a lease for space that required us to pay more rent per month than we had ever dreamed of making. We signed for the loan and put up all our furniture and car for collateral. Fortunately the bank didn't know the furniture was from the Salvation Army and the car was a $50 junker. We opened on a shoestring!*
>
> Flo Francis

With the bank's money in their account, they turned their attention to getting the space ready. This was a monumental task—the place was a wreck, it needed to be gutted and scrubbed, painted and more. In addition to themselves, they were joined by friends and Flo's theatre troupe. The theatre folk were all single and found it amusing that Joe and Flo, who were basically the same age as they were, already had three kids and were diving into this risky situation. They all dug in to help clean, paint and cheer the Francis team on.

The night before they were to open the new shop, while they were still cleaning and painting to get it just right, Flo discovered the bathroom hadn't been touched.

She'd later say "I had to go in there with a knife to scrape the crud off, it was just totally grungy. We finished up at 6:00 a.m. and rushed home to take showers, get dressed and be ready for our 'Grand Opening', just hours away. The renovation had taken weeks and we both lost 15 lbs. We looked like two skeletons but we were excited!"

During this renovation project, Flo had written to all the papers, put out flyers and used her considerable promotional talents to get all the publicity she could. They had gone up and down the street to invite all the other business owners to the opening for coffee and cake. Anyone passing by couldn't help but notice the ambition and passion Joe and Flo had for opening this business. Flo had offered reporters a free razor cut and all her efforts to get publicity had raised the bar for this "grand opening" to a fever pitch. In April of 1963, they opened their new salon, "The Village Barbers." All the hard work paid off, the turnout was terrific!

In anticipation of early success and being very busy, Joe had recruited another barber to take a chair and open with him. He solicited Marlin Stewart, a barber with a following of clientele, to manage a chair in the shop. He wanted a backup plan and figured Marlin would really help. Marlin had heard about this young guy who was going to do this crazy thing and had contacted him to buy his other two-man shop. Joe didn't want to sell and instead he convinced Marlin to come down and see what he was up to. Marlin checked it out and decided to take a risk and work for Joe in his new endeavor.

The plan was to have a first-class shop and they ordered six very expensive barber chairs and other equipment. Flo's friends from the theater, Jim Faber and Marlon Rodi, who were also artists, painted a large mural on one wall. Flo designed the shop to have mirrors above all the sinks along the entire length of the wall. She set up a special section for moms and kids to wait and decorated it with books, toys and child-sized seating. The renovation was impressive but it was a huge financial obligation and now it was time to hit pay dirt!

They decided to stick their necks out and try another angle. They invited local media people, athletes and community leaders (some of whom had been flying to New York City to get razor cuts) and gave them a free razor hairstyling. With the response they got, Flo built on the publicity and within weeks the shop was getting busy!

Back then, barbershops were not supposed to advertise. Joe was an active member of the Master Barbers Association, a self-governing and respected segment of the business. The organization had a standing rule that barbers shouldn't advertise. Joe didn't buy into this unwritten rule and decided to start some promotional advertising. The Association was run by some very traditional good 'ole boys. It didn't seem to bother them that barbers, at that time, lacked benefits, didn't get to take vacations and had no sick leave. Status quo was good enough for the governing body of the Association. Joe and Flo had put in tireless hours of volunteer work for them, always stepping up to work at the various Association events. Little did they know that they would create a stir when the new hairstyling shop in Highland Park started advertising. Joe didn't see the violation as anything more serious than a kid being ten minutes late for his evening curfew. There were many repercussions from the group even though independent barbers, at that time, were not doing well financially. They finally backed off when they saw that Joe's forward motion and leadership-by-example seemed to be benefiting the whole profession. Within a few short years they recognized Joe for his contributions to the whole business. In 1966, the AMBBA (Master Barbers Association) voted Joe Francis the *Upper Midwest Barber of the Year*.

Still, going from $1.75 to $5.75 per cut, at that time, was a struggle, but perseverance and tenacity once again paid off. Most of the barbering community though, just continued to watch.

The competition looked on and seemed frozen in their tracks. They were caught up in reactive behavior and cynicism; it'll never last—it's a fad—Francis went over the deep end this time—too bad for Joe. They looked on for five more years while The Barbers Hairstyling was becoming the only act in town, the only place you could get a razor cut. The competition stood still in time and followed the path of least resistance while Joe and his troops marched on. In fact, some of the competitors would make threatening calls; set up false appointments and called Joe and his crew fags, scabs and other debasing names. Later, many of the local barbers, who had been given a chance to join Joe and his team but declined, would admit they blew it—the parade just passed them by.

> *It's amazing! The customers show up in their big cars and fancy suits...people like Tarkenton, Applebaum, Gamble...all returning again and again. And they tipped us as much as the cost of the razor cut!*
>
> Joe Francis—1963

Before the grand opening, Joe was also looking for another seasoned barber who had a large clientele. He wanted to fill those chairs right out of the chute. One of his selections was a guy he pulled out of retirement, Jake Perlman, who had operated the biggest shop in St. Paul for years. Another was Joe's original barber school teacher, John Robida. But it didn't stop there; Joe hired a big hitter in the razor cut business to come in from Chicago and teach his barbers at night. This crew put in long, hard hours and their enthusiasm and penchant for the new concept never faded. It kept them all moving night and day.

Joe's selection process for barbers was as good as his flat top cuts. Jim Audette, Joe's first apprentice: "When I was in barber school, this guy would come in for a shave and a haircut. He had a really tough beard...the shave wasn't easy. Anyway, he kept coming back to me and I didn't know how significant this would be. Finally, one day he told me who he was and about his plans for the Highland shop. Then, he offered me a job!"

Through other industry contacts and business associates, Jim learned about Joe's reputation, popularity and about his involvement and success in the industry. Jim became Joe's first apprentice at the age of 18.

While all this was happening, Joe was also dedicated to other venues in the hair industry. In 1964, at the Upper Midwest Barber Show, Joe was one of the judges. A young barber, fresh out of barber school, signed up to compete. Joe checked the registration form, discovering the barber was only an apprentice and told him he couldn't compete; he had to be a Master Barber for the competition. They bantered back and forth but there was no way he could compete. The barber, Jeff Roberts, had just had his first encounter with Joe Francis—not a happy one. They would meet again in a couple years.

Meanwhile, Joe had his classy six-chair shop and five other barbers working beside him who were making really good money. Joe said later—"At the time of my Grand Opening, my net worth was a negative $5,000 and I wasn't able to draw a paycheck for three weeks but—we did make money that first year."

Have we arrived yet? Are we happy now? Not really. Joe thought: surely there's more—there must be more!

Overall, the Highland operation was doing well but Joe was getting the expansion itch—time to grow again. Looking for another affluent area, he decided to open a Salon in downtown Minneapolis. There were more professionals there; bankers, brokers, people in positions where personal appearance and style was critical. They also had higher incomes. Joe found a location and along with several of his barbers, would renovate the new Salon. They worked into the wee hours after they left the Highland shop each day. This was the process they followed for the next three shops as well—an inordinate amount of work!

Opening another shop also required Joe to start hiring again. The interviews were often less than ordinary. Tim Hawkins (who would become an important player later) remembers calling Joe for a job in the new Minneapolis shop. It wasn't open yet but Tim heard rumors it would be open soon. When he talked with Joe, Joe told Tim he'd like to meet the following Saturday. Tim told him that he was working all day and had plans to go to dinner and dancing that night. Joe responded that he'd be working in the new Minneapolis shop until late Saturday and Tim could come down afterward. Tim knew he wouldn't be free until 1:00 a.m. or so but Joe said that would work for him. They met at about 2:00 a.m. on Sunday morning and Tim was hired!

While Joe was still busy with his build-out in the Minneapolis salon, he conducted another evening interview. The candidate found him in overalls, putting up drywall and painting. The interview had been set up for late evening with this young barber who had a reputation for giving great haircuts and had mastered the "John-John" cut. This was a special haircut for kids following President Kennedy's assassination and the nation's exposure to his little son, John.

Joe had heard this barber was a hard working guy with a good reputation. Joe seemed to recognize him.

He asked several questions and then asked the candidate what his goals were. After he answered, Joe said "Well here's the most important question of all; do you want to open your own salon?" The barber confirmed "yes," at some point he wanted to open his own salon. Then Joe told him he wouldn't be able to use him. Joe needed loyal followers and didn't want any entrepreneurs coming on board. The young barber was Jeff Roberts, the very same man Joe had refused to let compete at an event a few years earlier. Jeff could have lied and might have been hired but it wasn't in his bones. As it turned out, it was probably best for both of them. Joe would catch up with Jeff again later.

The Minneapolis shop was going to be different. Joe's vision was sharper now and he had some new ideas. People always said that Joe was way ahead of the wave. This was more than a wave though; this would be a tsunami! Each hairstylist had a private booth, unheard of in a regular barbershop. Entering the shop on a long, red, very plush carpet, customers took a seat in expensive, black leather lounge chairs while they were waiting. Looking around, they couldn't help observing the authentic African animal skins that adorned the black walls. The customers responded with enthusiasm, and admired the stylists' uniforms—loud, striped shirts with black trousers. Joe had a penchant for putting his people in very stylish, trendy uniforms—something that made them all feel more professional.

These details were an intrepid move for Joe and his new approach was either going to bring 'em in or chase 'em out. It was Grand Opening time.

The start-up was a little slow—they got plenty of practice time on each other but very few customers. This lasted for several days and fortunately, Joe gave the stylists 100% of the take, just to keep them with him. Then one day, a customer came in for "the works." While he was there, he asked a lot of questions and the guys thought he was a little weird. What they didn't know was that this guy was a local reporter. He published a half-page article in the newspaper about the new shop, but alluded that perhaps "gay" barbers worked there. (None of them were gay.) The crew couldn't believe it! But, it did bring in a certain following of customers.

This reporter didn't know about the "Contender"—Joe Francis. Joe went right over to the rival Twin Cities newspaper and met with their most popular writer, Will Jones. Everyone loved Will's columns. Joe got him to sample a hairstyle, manicure and shoeshine and write an article too, but this time Joe and his Salon were sensationalized, and the article had an explosive impact. The paper hit the streets in November and from that time on, all Joe's stylists were booked solid from 8 a.m. to 6 p.m. daily. They couldn't even take time out for lunch!

The customers loved it! They not only came in, they lined up! Some may have come just to see the spectacle, but no matter, business was good—life was great—the customers were plentiful.

Executives, CEOs, athletes, race car drivers and other local celebrities, all continued to patronize The Barbers. The Twin Cities was home to the Vikings NFL team and sometimes ten or twelve would all come in at one time. Fran Tarkenton, Tommy Mason, Gary Larson and more would be regulars. Referrals came in droves. The Barbers was the only show in town!

With the phenomenal success of his two shops, Joe now had a new goal which was to dominate the Twin Cities market. He was staffed with many award-winning barbers and they advertised that fact. Enthusiasm continued to build among his staff and many of his stylists now had aspirations to manage the next location. They had been around Mr. Francis long enough to know that more was coming. Buzz Serber took over the Minneapolis salon. Jim Audette would take over another new one—the Midway salon. (The Midway is an area between Minneapolis and St. Paul.) There were three locations now and they were all run by award-winning barbers who would follow their charismatic leader in a heartbeat.

By this time, Joe had hired his cousin Bill Gabriel, who was a carpenter, to help in the build-out process for each new salon. Along with Bill, Joe's management team and stylists would all pitch in, working after hours on each new location. They would brainstorm regarding design colors, amenities and just get it done; cleaning, building, painting—whatever it took. There was no money available to hire contractors. Joe was right in the thick of the process along with his managers. During the expansion of the shops, Joe would sometimes make an impromptu call to Bill, telling him he needed work done at another location within a day or two. Joe was on a mission!

All the Francis children got involved in the business one way or another. Joey, the oldest of five, and John, the youngest, would get immersed in Joe's business in later years, and Susan, Jeanne and Barb, Joe's three daughters, got their taste too. As pre-teens, they were involved putting flyers out and worked on another of Joe's favorites, sidewalk sales in front of the salons. They'd solicit each passerby, selling hair products and a variety of other items. As teenagers, they often worked as receptionists in the salons and manned the Barbers MN State Fair booth. They also got put to work painting and cleaning in the new salon build-outs. Joe wanted them to learn what it was like to work for a paycheck.

As the tempo picked up at the Midway location, Joe hired a young man by the name of Earl Faulkner. He fit right in and started competing and winning in various competitions and Joe watched him carefully. Faulkner had been involved in a few shenanigans, (pranks that sometimes included customers) that upset Joe and in talking with Jim Audette and Marlin Stewart, he asked them "what're we gonna do with this guy? Are we going to fire him or should we give him a shop to manage?" Joe really had a "sixth sense" when evaluating people. He knew that given more responsibility, his employees would often raise the bar for themselves. Maybe Earl Faulkner was like that. After getting positive endorsements from Jim and Marlin, Joe decided to offer Earl the opportunity to manage his next location.

Many of Joe's barbers, co-workers and business associates through the years would say that one of the greatest gifts they ever got from this enthusiastic leader was confidence. Joe continually hammered the philosophy that *you can do whatever you set out to do!* Joe was a Champion! If he got knocked down, he was right back up and at it again. To Joe, failure was always nothing more than redirection. He'd often tell his colleagues, "We'll fail our way to success." When he was convinced that he could accomplish something, absolutely nothing stood in his way. And when things went wrong, he was never about fixing blame—he was about fixing the problem.

When young Faulkner got his big break, he learned something else about Joe Francis. When Joe turned over a location to a manager, he totally let go of the wheel. He expected them to do well and they did. He was extremely generous as well; often lending money to his managers for down payments on homes or for other pressing personal needs. Earl said years later, in an interview, "I jumped at the chance to manage and overnight I changed myself—literally changed overnight. The next day when I awoke, I was a completely different guy." Joe was right again; he trusted his gut instinct and made an enormous difference in Earl Faulkner's life. This was a difference that would shake the earth for Joe a short time later.

The Grand Opening for Faulkner's location, the Hillcrest salon, included a creative publicity stunt that Flo and Joe came up with. They would offer a free first haircut for six one year olds, including their one year old son, Johnny. Flo contacted the newspapers and radio announcers to see if they could cover the event. The media jumped on the idea and gave it a big spread in the newspaper as well as live radio and television broadcasts at the salon.

The company opened two more salons and by 1968, had five that were up and running. Abundant with passion and enthusiasm, Joe had the ability and vision to look far ahead. He knew this was going somewhere and knew he'd need a lot more barbers soon. No stranger to risk, in his selection process to find barbers who were hungry for success and more money, Joe recruited several right out of the St. Cloud, Minnesota Reformatory, a boy's detention center, which has a barber school. Many of those young men went on to become managers for Joe and most also came to purchase their own franchises. In fact, today several have become millionaires in the process.

Once his core group was trained, he set up training sessions for other local barbers. They were competitors but his crew trained them in the razor cut concept. Most of these barbers would opt to join Joe Francis and The Barbers, down the road.

Training was a critical, core element in the Joe Francis arena. As always, he led by example here too. In the earlier days of The Barbers, many of the training sessions were held in the homes of the various managers and stylists. They'd get together at 6:30 a.m. and Joe was always there. They also had other meetings in the evening and many of these loyal employees worked 10-hour, six-day weeks for over ten years. They became members of "The Founder's Club" (More on that later.)

This was fun and exhilarating but Joe could still see more. His dream was expanding and while he wasn't quite sure what was to come, he remained on the alert for new opportunities.

At the same time The Barbers was getting off the ground, television was on a huge growth track and shows were competing for all the human interest stories they could find. The Barbers concept *was* a find! On several occasions, the TV morning show, "This is the Place" featured Joe Francis with his apprentice, Jim Audette. Invariably, the phone would ring off the hook following these shows. Flo learned how to wring out every possible drop of publicity from events like this and continued operating the Public Relations department like a seasoned pro.

Competitive barbering events drew Joe in like metal filings to a magnet. At the 1963 International Barber Show in Manhattan, he won the coveted Global Award, placing second in the Worldwide Flat Top Championship. The first place went to a Japanese barber whom Joe and Flo visited in Japan later. Even though he had now immersed himself in the razor-cut concept, he continued to compete in this venue and his success would edify and support his building of a dream.

Earl Faulkner, was in awe of Joe and his talent. "At these competitive events, Joe would show up without a model—I mean, he would just pick a stranger from the crowd and demonstrate his skill. His cuts were so perfect, absolutely symmetrical—he was just incredible!"

This leadership by example set precedence for his stylists to compete as well. Nearly all Joe's trainees became national or international award winners, including his first apprentice, Jim Audette. Joe's tight-knit group actually formed a competition team that won awards all over the country, drawing even more attention to The Barbers.

It's not really clear whether Joe understood the impact this early success would have on what was to come. New customers were coming in from as far as ninety miles away. And Flo kept on developing new publicity ideas. She invited a local journalist who worked for a major paper to come in for a makeover. He took her up on it. Joe gave him a shampoo, razor cut, blow dry, eyebrow trim, shave, clay-pack facial and manicure. The session ended with newspaper photographers getting an "After" shot to compare with their "Before" shot. The next day, the journalist wrote: "Take the morning off and spend it at The Barbers. Pick a barber that swings with the times, a *hairstylist* instead of a barber."

Along with local media hype, the AP wire copy and major city newspapers all added fuel to The Barbers fire. After all, if you were going to get your first razor cut and style job, wouldn't you prefer to go to a salon with

National Award-Winning Barbers? With the continual company growth, there were always new hires. Being a customer service master, Joe had strict controls. He had his cousin, Tom George, act as a quality control consultant. He'd have Tom visit various salons for a haircut. Then Tom would get back to Joe and go over his experience at the salon, while Joe would check out the haircut. Tom would report on the condition of the salon, their customer service attitude and anything else Joe wanted to know. None of the locations knew they were being scrutinized and it turned out to be a valuable practice.

In 1964, Joe parted with his first barbershop, the location that started it all. He sold the small shop on Robert Street in West St. Paul to his longtime friend and first hire, Roy Oakes. Joe could have sold it many times over but he really wanted Roy to have it.

In 1966, while serving as Chairman for the Associated Master Barbers and Beauticians Association (AMBBA), Joe developed two new competitive events. These were introduced at the Association Convention in 1967. Joe, always an elegant dresser himself, with groomed hair, mustache and beard, saw this as a way to edify the hair stylist profession. His innate ability to see far ahead paid off again and these became annual events. The first was called 'Minnesota's Ten Best Groomed Men'. The second was 'Men's Hairstyling' and both were added to the competition agenda. The events went on to become hits with barbers, stylists, customers and media alike.

CHAPTER 3

THE FOUNDER'S MARATHON

The Barbers were now recognized as the consummate stylists, real "movers and shakers" in the industry. Joe had inspired this team to lead *with* him. They all looked to him for what was coming next and were ready to do whatever it required. This was a highly trained, workaholic team of National and International award winners, led by a charismatic CEO with very human bones who was right at the front lines with them. Would there be a *next* step or do they just bask in the sunshine of what had already been accomplished? Joe never quit reaching before and now he'd reach for more. But how? Maybe, he could take his concept and his company public—get a public offering going. With the money, he could expand in a major way. His company had gained local and national recognition;

why not go public? Maybe he should strike while the "iron was hot." Joe's accountant suggested he consider using a public offering as a stepping stone to going into franchising. Joe thought franchising was for hamburger chains, not for the hair business. But the more he thought about it, the more it piqued his interest. Franchising might be the answer?

A voracious reader of all types of business books, newspapers and magazines, he had read about and was impressed with the concept of franchising. Joe liked the business model concept and felt they had already built The Barbers "paradigm." With an influx of money, they could take The Barbers across the country. Franchising had caught on big both in the United States and internationally. The franchising concept had seen explosive growth in the 1950s and was still in an accelerated growth pattern during the 1960s, lead by the McDonalds restaurant giant. But in the 1960s, there were none in the hair care/beauty salon business. Investing in a franchise had proven to be a way to assure success and get to a healthy bottom line faster. It also held out a promise to be a safer investment versus private sector businesses.

Joe discussed his plan with Flo. She was skeptical and confronted him: "Joe, no one in the company has as much as a college degree, let alone experience in developing business plans and raising money. What about the legality of the undertaking? You should have lawyers and accountants. Joe, what are you thinking? Certainly you're not thinking about doing this on your own are you?"

Flo knew that he was incorrigible when he was on a mission, and she could read in his twinkling eyes, there was no way to stop him. The best thing she could do was learn all she could to support and help direct his plans. The plane was now on the runway, the throttle cranked to 115% of power, it was either going to lift off or crash! Flo continued to question Joe: "So, how do you get setup and what do people pay to own a franchise? What do they get for their money? Who do you sell them to?" Joe answered: "Well, Flo, you just do it. You just sell franchises. You get the money to get started from an initial public offering—it's that easy." Flo said: "OK Joe, but who's going to help you do this, how will you organize it?" She suggested they find competent counsel for this; a franchise attorney, a franchise marketing expert and someone to help write manuals and set up systems. But Joe planned to use whatever money he raised to do it *his* way. He didn't think it was such a big deal.

Imagine how tough it was for Flo. She was the "clean-up team" for so many of Joe's previous attempts at hitting a home run. It was always exciting but always challenging. Joe left an enormous vortex behind him; he'd put a 747 to shame in that category!

The type of Initial Public Offering Joe planned to use was limited to a top end of $300,000. Joe figured he'd need all of that to finance the company, set up his Marketing department and start selling franchises. (Flo later reflected that $3,000,000 would have been closer to the mark.) Little did he know at the time, his primary source of personal income, the following two years, would come from his real estate holdings. Through previous lean years, somehow Joe and Flo invested in fixer-upper homes they rented out. They had done very well with these investments and the income-producing property would now mean the difference between success and failure. It would have to support the family until the company was healthy. Joe had advised and mentored many of his management team about the value of investing in real estate. Most followed his lead and would tell you today it was one of the best financial moves they ever made.

Joe's team of *experts* were all barbers. They'd get together on a regular basis over the next few months to put the business plan in place, a requirement prior to making any stock offerings. Joe's excitement fueled their fires!

He was convinced he had enough contacts between his five shops and their clientele to raise the capital they needed. When customers were in the chair, the conversation invariably turned to the IPO, franchising and *getting in on the ground floor*. The recent significant publicity and success of award-winning barbers lent credibility to this new undertaking. Joe was right about raising the money. In March of 1969, they began soliciting for and sold out the IPO in weeks, long before the Underwriters completed the prospectus. They sold 100,000 shares at $3.00 per share. Customers who wanted to "buy in," actually got angry at many of the shop managers because the stock was sold out. In April, 1969, the stock began trading over-the-counter, it was lift off!

These securities having been sold, this announcement appears only as a matter of record.

NEW ISSUE

100,000 Shares

Common Stock

(Par Value $.10 per share)

THE BARBERS, HAIRSTYLING FOR MEN, INC.

Price: $3.00 per share

Copies of the Offering Circular may be obtained from:

THE BARBERS, HAIRSTYLING FOR MEN, INC.

1316-730 Building, 730-2nd Avenue South Minneapolis, Minnesota, 55402 332-0469

The original stock offering advertisement from the St. Paul Pioneer Press, Sunday, March 30, 1969.

People think I was driven by the money, fame or the prestige. None of that was important to me. Yes, it was nice. But to be able to accomplish what I set out to do was reward enough.

Joe Francis

While the IPO was in progress, rumors about Joe's intentions with the business were flying around within the barber community. Many of these barbers continued their jealous attacks. Joe sent out this letter to clear up the matter:

Dear Minnesota Barber/Stylist:

I am writing all licensed barbers in the State of Minnesota to inform you personally about myself and my company, The Barbers.

It seems there are individuals in our state spreading concern that small barbershops will soon be swallowed up by major corporations and large chains, and specifically, The Barbers. They claim there won't be anything left for the independent barber. Those of you, who know me, know how strongly I identify with the small shop operation. To those of you who don't know me personally, I will give you a brief resume.

I have been a licensed barber since 1952. I started out with a one chair shop, until I was able to add an apprentice, and I then I worked a two-chair shop for about 10 years. During all those years, I lived with the same problems common to all one and two chair shops. The problems I experienced prompted me to develop my multiple-shop corporation. I wanted to have the benefits other trades and professions enjoyed, which were not available to me as a barber. I set out to elevate myself and the industry. I wanted to have more than just a below average wage, which usually caused me to be regarded as a poor risk by bankers, with very limited income potential. I pioneered hairstyling, higher prices and professional policies.

I was criticized by my fellow barbers, as they were convinced it wouldn't work and were waiting for me to fail. When I didn't fail, but in fact succeeded in my work, many considered me a threat to the industry, because they were fearful of change.

By working so hard to establish a trend towards higher income and professionalism, I have helped to open the door for many of you who have also gotten the extra training, and extended yourselves to open a quality shop at tremendous expense.

My corporation was started in March of 1963 and since that time my thoughts and goals have not changed. It's ironic that after all these years of striving to elevate our profession; some barbers in Minnesota have been led to fear "Joe Francis and The Barbers."

In the process of building and sustaining all my shops, I have gained a wealth of knowledge and experience regarding our profession, which the small shop barber could use. All of you can benefit from my experience. I have been willing to help you avoid the mistakes I have made along the way, and I still am. The people that have joined me have benefited and that is pretty obvious. In fact, the people who have left me are also benefiting, by applying what they have learned. No, I'm not soliciting you to join The Barbers; I'm just trying to set the facts straight.

Very simply, I have set out to elevate myself and fellow barbers by developing the most professional hairstyling company in the nation. It is not my intention to destroy the industry but rather to make my children proud to say "my Dad is a barber," and know that being a barber in Minnesota is not anything less than any other professional job.

My company's success is tangible, in that our customers have come to rely on our professional service and we are very proud of the position the public has given us.

> Instead of fearing The Barbers growth, please realize we are offering prestige and security to the industry, proving that barbering is a business just like any other, with the potential to provide similar income and benefits. We are not keeping our marketing successes secret; on the contrary, we are anxious to help others achieve the goals we have already reached. Whenever any barbershop is a success, all barbers are elevated a notch.
>
> If you just stopped for a minute and divided the number of people in Minnesota by the number of barbers in Minnesota, you would see that there are more than enough for all of us. There will always be the one chair barbershop and there will continue to be the chains. There is plenty of room for both.
>
> Everyone has to work together to build a successful profession. We may be members of large organizations, small shops, the Board or the schools, but we're all the same, we're all licensed barbers.
>
> Don't you think it's time to look at what's happening, take a positive attitude, and resolve the problems we all have by dealing with them? We are all professionals, and true professionals, regardless of the size of their operation, will survive.
>
> (I enclose a brief information sheet to better acquaint you with my company.)
>
> Sincerely,
>
> Joe Francis

His letter helped and many local barbers felt better about The Barbers growth.

Most every successful entrepreneur has made and will make mistakes as they build their business. Joe was a risk taker and like most successful entrepreneurs, he too made some big mistakes as he built his business. Being a bargain hunter and always looking for a deal, Joe bypassed Flo's advice about hiring a franchise attorney and people with experience in raising money and franchising. He didn't like the idea of paying what was then "big money," for these services. This would come back to challenge him later.

All of this activity required more of Joe's time. He had quit cutting hair a year earlier and set up his new corporate office in downtown Minneapolis. It was a two-man office, small and cramped with Joe and his secretary, Patty Kessler. Patty reflects: "It was nice but so cramped, barely large enough for both of us. Then, two years later, Joe moved us into a less glamorous but larger space. There had been a fire in the building the year before and soot was all over the walls. There was 3-inch thick, green shag carpet, inadequate files and in whole it was a real contrast to Joe's polished appearance. It was a challenge—right above a sauna parlor and liquor store. We did get it cleaned up and in order though."

Apart from his ambitious plans to raise capital, Joe also wanted to develop his own private-label brand of hair care products. One of his managers, Bob Vaa, was promoted to Executive Vice President and appointed to get this done. Since the organization was too small to command the attention of any large manufacturer, Bob kept searching for a source but was facing continual rejection. With only five salons operating, the whole organization could only order six to twelve dozen products at a time—hardly enough volume to interest even the smallest manufacturer.

During his search, Bob came across a chemist who worked for one of the companies that had rejected The Barber's proposition. This chemist gave Bob some samples he had developed and told him to try them. After a short test and promising results, Bob went to Joe and told him he'd found a chemist who had some great products. They could hire him as their own in-house specialist for a $12,000 annual salary. "Won't work; we don't have that kind of money" says Joe. Bob told Joe about his unsuccessful search, he couldn't find products he liked and with the small orders they would place, he couldn't find a manufacturer that would supply them. "How about if I can make some kind of deal with this chemist," he asked "—are you behind it?" Joe gave him the go ahead, but only if he could make the products they needed, really good products for a low price.

Bob and another member of Joe's management team, Tim Hawkins, owned a small investment company called Tiro—"Ti" for Tim and "ro" for Robert. Most of their investing was in local stocks. Bob talked to Tim about investing in a private label products company along with Jim King, the chemist he'd met. The three of them got together and decided they'd invest $200 each to form "Tiro Industries." They found a small office they could rent for $60 a month. Their new laboratory consisted of a 4x8 sheet of plywood atop two saw horses and it included a small bathroom. Each night after work, the three men would get together. Jim would bring five-gallon pails of his concoction and they'd transfer it to pitchers for pouring into their retail containers. This created quite a mess! As luck would have it, there was a bathtub in the bathroom, where they could rinse off the retail bottles. Bob loaded the finished product into the trunk of his car for delivery to the salons the next day. This humble start would later play into the salvation of Joe's company.

In the earlier days, The Barbers core group was a bunch of wild and crazy guys, barely out of their teens. Far too often, Joe would have to reprimand them for their shenanigans in the various shops. He could tolerate some of it but if it affected a customer, he blew a fuse!

These were just *small* things; like the time one of them removed a part from his fellow stylist's clippers. This resulted in a 'customer standup'—(a move done when one gets the nape of their neck caught in the teeth of a clipper). Of course the customer blamed the stylist. Revenge was in order. The violated stylist noticed his associate leaving for lunch and he rushed next door to the grocery, bought some Limburger cheese, came back, dismantled his partner's blow dryer and packed the cheese inside next to the heating element. The violator returned from lunch to find his next customer waiting. After a masterful cut, he began to finish with his comb and blow dryer. Phew! The man jumped up, ripped off the cape and stormed out. When that customer left, the door had to be open for a long, long time. Joe heard about this and drove right over to the salon to read them the riot act. Joe loved to have fun, but never at a customer's expense.

There was another situation where one of the stylists thought his associate was sitting in the next barber chair reading and waiting for a customer. (The stylist couldn't see over the divider between the chairs.) So, the prankster soaked some towels in cold water and tossed them over the divider, fully expecting them to hit his fellow barber. Not quite, they landed on the head of his associate's customer.

Some of these pranks were funny, but some were outrageous. One of the stylists thought it would be pretty funny to pull a nylon stocking over his head, load a gun with blanks and come into one of the salons, when no customers were present, to pull off a fake hold-up. He did exactly that, forcing the manager and another stylist to the floor and firing off a couple blanks for effect. The victims were terrified! If there had been a security guard or policeman walking by, the prankster could have been shot himself; not too bright! This was one prank that Joe never learned about until much later. It's anyone's guess as to whether the prankster would have been fired if Joe had known about it at the time.

But Joe and his barbers evolved into serious businessmen. They began getting together on a regular basis, every week, to organize the franchise start-up. They held their meetings in Jim Audette's basement. Present were: Joe Francis, Jim Audette; Marlin Stewart; Tim Hawkins; Buzz Serber; Earl Faulkner and Bob Vaa. They had raised the money to form a franchise company. Now they needed a Franchise Operations Manual, training aids, guidelines, marketing plan, budgets etc. They eventually pulled it all together. It could have been better but this was a start.

At this point, Flo was still pushing for a professional team to come on board and organize the franchising effort. Joe realized he was in over his head and did hire a few *so-called* franchise pros. However, he didn't pay enough to get seasoned, successful help. The result was a financial tragedy. For one thing, Joe tried a shotgun approach for setting up franchises. He was personally all over the country, pitching his concept and sharing his success story. But he forgot one important piece of the puzzle. The Barbers had super credibility in the upper Midwest where almost everyone had heard their story. But they were not a household name elsewhere.

Joe thought California and the East Coast would both be super markets. However, when he took his story to these markets, no one knew about him or The Barbers. Joe was a good salesman. He was always dapper—in tailored suits and fancy shoes. He was a handsome man with thick, black, wavy hair, precisely trimmed beard and moustache. He moved with confidence and energy. What was more important though was his sincerity. He could sell a story. Franchises were purchased and opened but there was no impetus to push them forward.

Lacking the credibility the Minnesota shops enjoyed, these distant franchises did not do well and many needed more supervision than there was staff to provide. Miles of time-consuming travel and expenses were eating up the cash. The nest egg from the IPO was dwindling. Nevertheless, Joe had his five original shops in Minnesota and new franchises in Pennsylvania, Nebraska, Michigan and California. However, the vault was nearly empty and some of these shops were not turning a profit.

Joe's bookkeeper, Vi Demos, always monitored his spending and sometimes had to hide the checkbook from Joe. Little more than a year had gone by since the IPO and the cash was running out. Not everyone embraced Joe's optimistic outlook. It was getting bad. Bankruptcy loomed in the background and it was time for an emergency meeting. Joe would have to inform his management team about the dire situation. He didn't look forward to it. He'd often hide the worst news from Flo and this was one of those times. She did know the checkbook was getting thin but not that the company was in danger of shutting down. In situations like this, Joe used to say "what's the worst thing that could happen—that we go broke? Well, I've been there; done that—we'll still be OK." Flo wasn't afraid either, they had been on many adventures together and had more to come. She was every bit the trooper Joe was and they were always in it together!

At the meeting with his loyal, workaholic staff, Joe said: "Well boys, I've got bad news for you. We've only got enough cash to make our current payroll and then we're out of money." He appealed to his team "anyone have an idea that might save us?" Joe did have an open mind; he wasn't in a locked-up-ego state and he would often accept unsolicited input. He was also an excellent listener. Earl Faulkner stood and said "What if the salons could double or triple the cosmetic sales, would that save the company?" The company accountant, Joe Demos, worked the numbers and said it might work, if they could pull it off.

Faulkner, who would later become one of The Barbers greatest success stories, had been managing a shop on St. Paul's East side. Looking for ways to bolster his profits, in a working-class neighborhood where the $5.75 razor cut price was a little steep. He had enrolled in a nine month Sales Training course. Earl believed that if he wanted to provide good service for his customers, he had to make their hair look better with products they could use at home. Earl trained his staff, who emulated this philosophy, and soon products were going out the door nearly as fast as they came in. This had an immense, positive impact on his bottom line. Joe asked all the salon managers if they'd be willing to train with Earl and get things in motion. "I was still earning my bread and butter cutting hair" Earl said, "but I'd leave my shop Friday nights, head for the airport and fly to a location for a product training session. These would sometimes last up to midnight. I'd head out Saturday morning for the next location and so on. On many occasions, I'd return home just hours before I opened my shop on Monday morning."

Years later, in an article for *Minnesota Business Journal*, Joe, reflecting on that meeting, wrote: "Fortunately for me, the boys rallied. They wholeheartedly believed in The Barbers and pledged to make it work. We had only a short time to make it work but we all left that meeting believing we could do it." Several of Joe's early managers described him as a 'Pied Piper,' wherever he went we'd follow."

How many business leaders, finding themselves in a position like this, could earn such profound respect that their employees would work endless hours, train even more hours and retain their professional composure at the same time? Joe (always a leader by example) and his team, were getting right in the face of impending disaster.

Faulkner remained loyal to the cause, training salon owners every weekend for months. After every training session, product sales would pick up the following week and Joe would keep Earl posted on sales receipts, often thanking him again for his dedication and efforts.

Because the company was nearly broke at the outset of this effort, Joe had to convince their private label product manufacturers, Tiro Industries, to carry them until they could start repaying. Bob Vaa, was still on The Barbers management team and one of the owners of Tiro. Bob: "I had to mortgage my house and borrow money from my father-in-law to carry the company but we hung together like glue." The tab ran up to $135,000 before repayment kicked in. Bob Vaa was a godsend but betting on Joe and his dream was no problem for him.

Thanks to his association with The Barbers, Bob grew the beauty products business and eventually bought out his two partners. He left his management position with The Barbers in 1977 and expanded his business to ultimately operate in a 450,000 square foot building with 400 employees and revenues over $70 million annually. Like Joe, Bob was from a poor background; his success, to be sure, warmed the heart of Joe Francis.

Meanwhile, Joe went to his lawyer's father, Ralph Stacker, to arrange a loan to pay off past-due construction costs. With only his real estate holdings to sustain him and his family, Joe would forego 15 months of salary. He even gave one of his personally owned, most profitable salons, to the new publicly owned company he had formed, to keep it afloat. With commitment, perseverance and tenacity, Joe was not going to fail, he would succeed. His incredible performance and that of his staff saved the company and they never lost a single shop or had to cut anyone's salary. Joe's was the only salary that suffered. His $18,000 per year stopped on June 1, 1970 and didn't start again until October, 1971. His salon managers and stylists were making more money than Joe was. Indeed, his vision was what kept him going. He wasn't looking for a base hit, he was chasing the "Home Run."

At that time, The Barbers was the only franchised chain of hair salons in the country. Despite all the self-created problems the company was experiencing, they were still in a positive mindset. Thanks to Joe's leadership style, his stylists' advice and endless loyalty, the company was way ahead of the curve in their industry.

Competitive events in the Barber and Hairstyling industry, no matter who sponsored them, drew Joe Francis in like a moth to a flame. He didn't just come to compete—he was there to win! No sooner had a new barber or stylist joined The Barbers, when Mr. Francis would be talking to them about competing. Some of his associates would compete in spite of a case of severe nerves. Earl Faulkner once said he was terrified going into his first competitive event. He said the guys he was competing against were formidable, to say the least. He said that even though he was frightened half to death, in no way would he let his leader down and he sent in his entry. On the day of the event, *The Stephen Barberama of 1967,* Earl experienced tremendous, crippling back spasms. He hung in there though, just as he knew Joe would have if he was having the same problem. Earl won first prize in both of the events he entered.

Joe loved competing himself and if *he* ever had a case of nerves, it certainly didn't show. He encouraged all his Barbers to compete; to "get in there and show 'em what you've got." Joe's encouragement for his associates to compete was not just about being in the game. He knew that no matter where they placed in a competitive event, it would raise their confidence and self-esteem levels. He loved seeing others achieve and feel good about themselves. He could hardly have known in the earlier years, how valuable their winning records would become.

During the 1967 Barber Convention in Minneapolis, a long black Cadillac pulled up and out stepped Joe and several of his "boys." All were dressed to the "nines," wearing suits with their shoes shined, and reeking of confidence as they strode into the hall. Heads turned—other barbers querying each other about who these guys were.

They found out in short order. During the styling competition, Jim Audette, Buzz Serber and Tim Hawkins won First, Second and Third place respectively. This was significant, as over 1,000 barbers would attend these shows and there were hundreds of competitors. Through the following years, The Barbers hair stylists won hundreds of local, national and international awards. The three biggest national and international award winners were Joe Francis, Gil Gilbertson and Bill Kaminski. This brought publicity no one can buy and it made its way to the media. Newspapers, radio announcers and TV news coverage continually ran stories on these accomplished hair stylists.

CHAPTER 4

TIME OUT

In spite of the marathon pace he created, Joe would occasionally find time for a couple of his favorite pastimes; hunting and fishing. He was an avid and successful hunter who would venture out to Alaska, Montana, and the Dakotas, hunting big game and big fish. Joe and some friends had converted an old school bus that served as a camper and rolling hunting lodge. Flo remembers a phone call from Joe, "I'm in Montana, the bus broke down and I need you to send $260, so we can get back on the road." He was also a collector of fine shotguns and loved to go pheasant hunting.

The *boy* in Joe's interests was enjoyed by the neighborhood kids along with his own children. He bought an antique fire truck for parade use and would often take all of them for several laps around the block. Joe also loaned-out his prize truck to franchisees to use in their local area parades. He was intrigued with magic and often gathered all the kids together to mesmerize them with his magic tricks. He was pretty good at it too. He was one of the first in the neighborhood to get a snowmobile and the nearby lake, when frozen, became a playground for son Joey, his siblings and his buddies. At one time, Joe had a vehicle collection that included a 1940 fire truck, a 1955 Thunderbird, 1919 Ford Model T, a 1930 Model A, and 1973 Cadillac convertible.

Joe was forever attracted to gadgets and unusual inventions. Flo remembers the day he came home with an automatic potato peeler. This thing was the size of a big drum, no doubt intended for use in a huge cafeteria or the military. Joe just beamed: "Look Flo, you just throw potatoes in it, turn it on and it automatically peels hundreds of potatoes!" Flo wanted to know what would require her to peel hundreds of potatoes?

He was always at the front of the line when a new concept hit the market and was also one of the first to own a microwave, CB radio, Pong video game, car cell phone, VCR and phone answering machine.

For many years, Joe was in the habit of wearing a different watch everyday. He told one of his business associates that wearing a good-looking watch was important for an enterprising businessman. He'd continue to do this until Flo gave him a Rolex. She knew he'd treasure it. In order to purchase this special gift, from time to time she'd tell Joe she spent $100 on groceries when it was really $70 or $80, and she'd save the difference. Flo did this until she could buy him the Rolex as a

Christmas gift. The whole family watched as Joe opened his gift. They would never forget the look on his face when Flo told him it was an *authentic* Rolex. He wore only that one watch from that day on.

Joe also acquired a special custom trailer that came with one of the antique cars he purchased at an auction. It was put together with some hard-to-find parts. Bob Sausen, Joe's personal CPA and accountant, had become a friend of Joey Francis. One day, Sausen needed a trailer to haul some dirt out of his yard. Joey told him he had it covered; he had a trailer and they could dump the dirt on Joey's land. The trailer was Joe's little pet trailer and he was very proud of it. On the way to Joey's property, with the loaded trailer, they blew a tire and ruined the rim as well. Bob said, due to the age of the rims, he had to make about ten calls to junkyards to find a match. They knew they had to tell Joe what happened. Joe would be shattered if his pet trailer was harmed. So they got it repaired and when they told Joe it was all OK again, he was really grateful. Bob said "this was a huge deal to him. With all the other stuff going on, he was still worried about the little trailer."

Joe's grandchildren all called him "Buppa" and they called Flo "Nana." Joe loved playing with his grandkids and he built a little playhouse for them that even had a loft and wooden tulips outside the windows. The grandkids thought it was great having tea parties in their playhouse. Sarah Goldstein, Susan's daughter, remembers a day when Joe was babysitting and told them "time for some cereal." When he discovered there was only chocolate milk in the fridge, he used that and told the kids it was good for them. They all loved spending time together with Buppa and Nana.

At one point, Joe's daughter Susan, and her husband Jeff, moved to England with their children. Sarah, the youngest, recalls Joe and Flo coming to visit and Joe jumping on the trampoline with them. It was near an apple tree in the backyard and Joe was trying to jump high enough to try and snag some apples. Sarah also recalls a song they learned from Flo, who has a great sense of humor. The lyrics: *I love Nana—Nana is beautiful—more beautiful than a movie star—younger than springtime and as skinny as a rail—eyes as green as grass—lips as red as rubies—skin as soft as satin and teeth as white as pearls. I love Nana who always brings lots of smiles.*

Benji Francis, Joey's son, has a lot of fond memories of time spent with Buppa. Benji says Buppa was always happy and positive. The two went ice fishing together on the lake where Joe's house was located. It was nothing fancy. They sat on buckets and enjoyed their day together. Benji said he always felt safe with Buppa and Buppa always knew what to do.

The Francis family spent 23 years in their home on Lake Gervais in the St. Paul suburb, Little Canada. Living there was one of Joe's longtime goals. As a young boy, he often fished near the public beach and he clearly remembered the beautiful home on the point of the lake's peninsula. Joe dreamed he would one day own a home like that on Lake Gervais. It must have been a goal and not a dream. Years later, he moved the family out of the house that he and Flo had built five years earlier and into that very dream house on the lake. But the move was not easy. Although the home offered great potential, it was in tough shape when they bought it. They had to expend a great deal more time, energy and money to get it where they wanted it. Flo hired a friend of Joe's, Art Nassef, a talented, St. Paul building contractor. Art customized all of Flo's designs, room by room as he gutted them out and then built on additions. The whole project was arranged by a handshake, testimony to the integrity of the Francis family and to the trust they had in Nassef. He completed everything quickly and professionally, all to Flo's delight. Although it was stressful during the renovation project, there were many more renovations and alterations in the years to follow.

Joe bought a pontoon boat and many management meetings took place on it. Since he and Flo loved to entertain, the lake home turned out to be a perfect setting for their legendary parties. They had a Christmas party every year, one for friends and relatives, and one for business associates. They loved to have a full house, with dancing, music and good cheer for everyone. They always had a blast! The Christmas parties were a spectacle.

Family friend, Grace Gallagher: "That Flo! I remember Christmas Day less than a month after her son John was born and Flo insisted on having their traditional Christmas Party and Open House. I was always amazed at how the couple could entertain during the busy holiday season. There was always good food and drinks but we'd always celebrate the birth of Jesus with a birthday cake."

Family friend, Doyle Glass: "I'm not going to say that's where the party *always* was, but if anything was going on in the neighborhood, Joe and Flo were usually part of it. The two would entertain in grand style, and Joe, who loved to cook, would often serve gourmet meals. There was a special party or celebration held on every holiday at the Francis home, it was a family tradition."

Flo reminisces, "When the kids were younger, we had their little friends come in on a Saturday afternoon for a special Christmas party and Santa Claus came to hand out gifts. Our big family bash started on Christmas Eve and didn't end until very late Christmas Day. First we went to church early in the evening on December 24th, then returned home. We'd get all dressed up in our costumes. I had lots of white choir robes to fit any size, along with halos and wings to fit many sizes of Angels. I also had long, beautiful priests' robes for the Wise Men, along with turbans and crowns. For the Shepherds and for Mary, Joseph and Jesus, we had long blue and white robes with surplices. Of course the baby Jesus rested on a golden fabric, with a white and gold covering and a white feather halo above him. In 1966, the year John was born, we had him be the baby Jesus, when he was just one month old. (The family still celebrates this nativity pageant every year.)

"Our Christmas Eve pageant is a candlelit reading of gospel and singing Christmas hymns, beautifully played by son-in-law Jeffrey Goldstein. We end up kneeling before Jesus (our youngest grandchild) and sing *Silent Night*, adjourning to Jesus' birthday cake and singing *Happy Birthday*. It is very meaningful and tons of fun.

"On Christmas Day, while Joe was alive, we always had an Open House party that began at about 4:00 p.m., for all our friends and relatives and their children. This was really a large gathering and the food and drink flowed, along with lots of music and dancing until about midnight. It was always a lot of fun and all the friends and relatives got to know each other very well, over the years."

Besides the family parties, there was an annual Corporate Christmas Party, a gala dinner, dance and banquet that was held at a large hotel in Minneapolis. All office personnel, franchisees, vendors and others attended. There was always a dance band and convention-style banquet set-up and everyone came 'dressed-to-the-nines'. A lot of awards were given out, covering about twenty categories of outstanding achievement among the franchisees around the country. In the last few years, 600-700 people attended this event.

We also had an annual Sunday Brunch for the Board of Directors and top Management personnel at our home. Flo had this catered with a large smorgasbord and refreshments passed by waiters. One year, this event was featured in a magazine article.

An office Christmas party, held at the corporate office, was another gathering where the office personnel received thanks along with their annual bonus checks. The staff also exchanged "secret Santa" gifts, handed out by Scott Schnieder, who dressed as Santa Claus.

The annual company picnics were held at a large, reserved section of a public park in St. Paul or Minneapolis. These were day-long events, attended by all the franchisees and home office staff and their families. There were lots of games for all the kids and adults, which included a softball game, wheelbarrow races, lots of water balloons and egg-throwing contests. Prizes were awarded and food was abundant. One year they roasted a pig and there were always kegs of beer, abundant food and a lot of fun taking place.

CHAPTER 5

BACK TO WORK

The years 1970 and 1971 were antagonistic to the Barber industry in general. Trade journals reported a 40 percent decline in the business and most independent barbers lagged behind, they hadn't jumped on the "products" bandwagon or the razor-cut concept and they couldn't survive. Somewhere in the neighborhood of 30,000 barbershops were closing yearly. Considering this climate and the financial woes of The Barbers franchise group, their ultimate success story is even more remarkable.

About this time, a trend, influenced by The Beatles and their longer hairstyles changed men's hair fashions. This revolution caused men to stop going to barber shops and instead, go to women's styling salons, where the beauticians knew how to cut long hair. The Barbers were at the forefront of this trend and created some of the first and most successful "Uni-sex Salons" in the country. Men were now interested in hair coloring as well. Franchise owner, former salon manager and trainer, Charlie Brown, recalls: "The shag hairdo had become popular for men. We were doing such a great job with the guys—it drew women in too. We trained our stylists to do permanents, hair color and the new styles so we could service both male and female customers."

As Joe had said, "If traditional barbers don't change with the times, they'll miss out on a dramatic boom in both product sales and the cross-over male/female business." This was prophetic. Statistics for failing barber shops were staggering. Joe had a hard time understanding the mind set of these stay-behind barbers. Joe was always willing to stick his own neck out and one time he decided to be the Guinea pig for a hair coloring session. He went to The Barbers salon in Minneapolis, managed by Tim Hawkins. Joe handed Tim some black hair coloring and peroxide and said "color my hair." Tim said he'd never colored anyone's hair. Joe said "it's easy, just do it."

Tim recalls—"With Joe, everything was always *easy*." Tim mixed up the coloring and peroxide and vigorously rubbed it into Joe's hair. Joe's hair was now pitch black but so were Joe's ears, forehead and the perimeter of skin around his hairline. Tim, in a near panic, called one of his best clients, Gordon Locksley, whom he knew could tell him what to do. Gordon had been coloring his own hair for years. He told Tim to use cigarette ashes, rub them into the skin and wipe them off. It worked! With Joe, customer service was paramount. He would never subject any customer to a procedure he wasn't sure about. Joe, always leading by example, also wanted his stylists to learn to step out of their comfort zone, when the situation would warrant it.

With the increasing product sales and adjusting to the changing needs for hair care, The Barbers sales, as reported in Annual Corporate Report, went from $357,617 in 1970 to $868,608 in 1971. They also trimmed operational costs and the 1970 deficit of $122,196 was reduced to $26,166 in 1971. From nearly failing, the company was coming out of the woods and had some light at the end of the tunnel.

The company learned an important lesson in 1970. By opening too many corporate salons, fast growth led to a lack of control. They opened just three salons in 1971. At fiscal year end, June, 1971, they had fifteen corporate stores in six states and two franchise shops; one was located in Duluth, Minnesota and the other in Omaha, Nebraska.

Someone buying a franchise from The Barbers in 1970 would invest about $37,500 to earn from $6,000 to $8,000 annually. They could earn more if they were also a stylist working in their own franchise. *The Barbers* corporate hair stylists were making from $14,000 to $25,000 annually, without investment or debt! Joe felt that the best franchise operators would come from his core group of managers. They were proven, worked countless hours, were loyal to the cause, believed in their concept and also in Joe. He wanted all of them to experience the pride of owning their own business. The problem was they were making more money as stylists, than a single franchise owner. But, they could do much better if they owned and expanded their own business like Joe had done. Consistent with his lifelong dream to make a poor man rich, this mission had an underlying strategy as well. Looking at the McDonald's franchise paradigm, with multiple locations controlled by a single franchisee, Joe could see his company emulating that structure. He knew these hardworking winners would win even bigger if they owned a larger slice of the pie. In addition, his company would win too. If these Managers could each own and expand to about five salons and maximize sales, there was the upside chance they could net over $200,000 per year. In his President's Report to the stockholders in 1972, he wrote: "Because of our determination to establish a firm financial base for the company, we limited our expansion almost exclusively to franchised shops. And during this past year, many leading shopping center developers and hotel chains contacted us. Because of this unsolicited interest in our franchising program, we anticipate expanding to other states in the coming years."

Besides his unending faith in his "boys," as Joe lovingly called his management staff, he had a deep seated belief that women would do well in his franchise system. It was in 1971, while attending a Beauty/Barber show in NYC that Joe would meet the first female stylist he recruited to his company. A young lady was attending the show—a single mom who was fresh from Barber school. Joe told her to enter the Cutting competition along with his staff. She didn't think she was good enough because she had no experience to back her up and women were not readily accepted in the barbers' world. Women were expected to be beauticians or cosmetologists. Joe insisted, "C'mon, you can do it! Sign up—let's go." She finally gave in and went over to the registration desk to sign up. They turned her down at the desk because they didn't believe she was a barber. Joe overheard this and stepped in.

Joe: "Hey she's not a beautician—she's a barber. You have to let her cut."

They retort: "No way, she's not gonna cut."

Joe: "Oh really? Well she's gonna cut or I'm going to start a lawsuit against you—she's going to compete." They finally accepted her.

The young mom, Peggy Schmidt, hailed from Boston, Massachusetts. She had street smarts and a good intellect as well. Later, she went to work for Joe in a Radisson Hotel salon, and became an outstanding, model stylist and business woman.

Another incident demonstrates the loyalty Joe showed his employees. A wise guy used to frequent the salon where Peggy worked. He would make demeaning remarks to her in front of her associates and the customers. One day, she'd had it. She told him she was no longer going to cut his hair and to find another stylist. The customer called Joe to report on her. Joe listened to the story—it was the first he'd heard of this and when the customer was finished, Joe said, "Tell you what—that strikes me as unusual because she will cut anybody, anytime—lunch hour, early, late—there must be some reason she won't cut your hair. So here's what you need to know—not only do I not want you to go back to her salon; I don't want you to go to any of my salons, because if she doesn't want you, none of us want you either."

Peggy Schmidt, whom Joe now called "Scrappy," was totally customer-oriented. Her hard work and extra hours took her to the top of The Barbers' organization. Her first year with them she earned the coveted "President's Club" award. Peggy went on to become the first woman in the United States to ever be a Barber Board member. Years later, she attempted to open her own Barber school and was turned down. She had to fight Twin Cities' school owners and their attorney and it was rough. She asked Joe for his help. He showed up and approached the governing body at a public hearing, "If anybody can run a Barber school, it will be this woman." He continued his presentation in support of Peggy and she got her license to open the school.

No doubt, it was the advice and support Joe got from Flo, his recognition of her many talents, her efforts and performance in the face of adversity that influenced his attitude about women. In later years, 30% of his Franchisees were women. In addition, the corporation was recognized nationally and rated the #1 Minnesota public company in the area of utilizing women for board directors, corporate officers and staff in 1997.

The growth of store openings came to a standstill in 1972 but every month sales increased and revenue jumped significantly from the $868,608 of 1971 to $1,317,925 in '72. The company bought the Harrisburg Barber School in Pennsylvania in 1972. This was a strategic move to recruit and train stylists for future growth and it proved to be a good move. Joe's interest in acquiring Barber schools was driven by his customer service ethic. If they had more control in the training process, the company would have superior stylists. He also knew there would be a shortage of barbers for franchisees to hire if he wasn't proactive.

By the end of 1973, his school had doubled its enrollment and had doubled its economic value. More important was the fact that the company became more selective and cautious in their franchisee and site selections. They didn't open any new locations until the fourth quarter. In the fourth quarter, they opened four corporate and five franchise shops and had year end revenue of $1,857,621—up $540,000 from the 1972 number. By year end 1974, they had 34 salons operating and revenue had increased to nearly $2.5 million. Product sales were up over 35%. Joe must have been thinking about the day in 1970 when he called that dismal meeting and life was pumped back into the company. Thanks to Earl Faulkner and his relentless effort to help turn things around and to Tim Hawkins and Bob Vaa at Tiro Industries, the company was moving in a positive direction again.

CHAPTER 6

FRANCHISE GROWTH

Things were improving and the treacherous learning curve wasn't quite so tight. Joe felt he was still on the right track, with franchise survival statistics being far superior to private, independent business. The franchise business claimed a 95% success rate during the first 5 years from opening. A less-than 20% survival rate was the norm for non-franchise ventures. Obviously, if you were looking for your own business and had to make a serious financial investment, you'd prefer some likelihood of success. Going with a proven idea would be the choice for many entrepreneurs.

However, these "A" type franchise owners often wanted to change parts of the system and far too often, the parts they changed were the most integral to success and were those that made it work. The selection process was being re-evaluated by Joe. The idea of getting his managers, those that already had a proven track record, into their own franchises became ever more important to him. However, the shotgun approach Joe had taken earlier, setting up franchises wherever the interest came from, continued to stretch management. Problems were developing at some of the California salons.

In 1974, Tim Hawkins took over management of the salon in the St. Francis Hotel, Union Square, San Francisco. This was a big salon with 10 stylists and 3 shoeshine stations. It was situated downstairs, far below street level, and was one of several that were not ideally located. Sales were down at this locale and Joe needed a seasoned manager to get it on track. The clientele was upscale, varied and included movie stars and hotel guests from all over the world. Some of the celebs that came were Truman Capote, Ricardo Montalban, Raymond Burr and Karl Malden, to name just a few. There were high-powered egos to deal with and some hotel guests would not have their hair done in the salon, they required that the stylist come to their rooms. It took Tim seven months to get this salon profitable and as usual, the job got done and the salon was sold to a new franchisee.

It was in this period that the company hired Tom Tweed to do market research. His first assignment was to prove the need for higher student enrollment in barber schools. Joe saw a serious shortage of barbers and stylists in the coming years. He knew he'd have to present overwhelming evidence to the powerful State Board, before they'd consider an increase in enrollments. Tom took months collecting data. He had numbers for the chairs needed, total student population, parking spaces required and consumer opinions that proved customers' needs were not being met.

His findings were presented in court to provide evidence for the need to increase enrollment. The judge didn't understand marketing concepts, what "median" meant or how calculations were made. It took several hearings over several months. The opposition included barbers who spoke out against more competition. Even though they had no real evidence to support their position, their testimony was damaging to The Barbers cause. There were no laws to prevent one barber from opening a shop close to another one. So, to prevent more competition, the other barbers tried to slow down the training process.

This really got Joe's ire up and he encouraged Tweed throughout the process to hit 'em hard! Tom was successful and this opened the doors to more school openings and the expansion of existing schools. Joe remained passionate about the need for Barber Schools but not just *any* school. He wanted young people to get the very best of training and be inspired to see the trade as a profession. He knew that if he could turn out students from his schools with that mindset, the industry overall would improve. Joe went on, in later years, to open six entry-level barber schools while building the company.

To increase awareness for The Barbers brand, Tweed began to step up business advertising. He set up a company sponsored skate board park at the Minnesota State Fair. A campaign called "The Big Kahuna," ensued, and various salons gave away skate boards. More TV ads were developed, wrapping around a theme "What A Change." These visual-verbal ads pointed out that a positive change took place in a person's appearance after a visit to The Barbers. Joe's company was the only chain in the country advertising like this at the time. The success of these ads gave the company huge impetus and brand recognition in the markets where these ads were run.

By fiscal year end 1975, the company owned 41 salons that were staffed by 210 stylists. They owned three Barber Schools, located in California, Illinois and Pennsylvania. They also had 15 franchise owners now. But attention to growth and services had distorted the focus. Franchising and being a franchiser, brings with it myriad legal details. You have to be on top of all your legal responsibilities. In March of 1976 the company failed to register their Agreement with the State of Minnesota. In compliance with the Department of Commerce, Securities Division and Federal Trade Commission, The Barbers had to suspend all new franchise sales until they remedied the registration. This was crippling, financially, but not life threatening. It gave them a breather and time to fine-tune other important matters. Four months later, they were selling franchises again, lessons being learned.

Joe was in the process of another costly, bitter lesson about the importance of hiring credentialed business professionals to run the Corporate office. He believed that anyone who was motivated to succeed could do anything. This proved to be too optimistic. Who knows where they would have been at that point if he had listened to Flo's advice about hiring experienced professional help—certainly in a better financial condition!

Many of the staff in control were barbers and salon managers. They didn't have the necessary business background and skills required for a company of this magnitude. This created expensive "fixing" and damaged the bottom line. When the franchisees didn't follow the system, they lost money and so did the home office. Monitoring the operations and the actions of franchisees was very costly and time-consuming, especially when they were so widely spread out.

Still, the company achieved record sales in 1977. Their revenue rose to over $4,900,000, an increase of 23.4% over 1976. Income from franchises was up 128% over the prior year. The Barbers stood at 29 company shops and 34 franchises. Cosmetic sales bridged the $1,000,000 mark and the school's tuition numbers were up as well. Joe's 1977 Report to The Shareholders boasted the company's highest pre-tax income to date. Their tireless efforts to provide new programs and support for franchise owners had paid off.

This was all happening in the face of other competition from regional and national brands like Regis, Fantastic Sams, Great Expectations and Command Performance.

Management positions were being developed and tighter controls on franchise operations were improving the whole system. A once chaotic atmosphere was losing its choking grip and the system was breathing better. Managers Marv Alvheim and Charlie Brown accepted key management positions at home office and as always, they dug in—putting in countless hours to get the job done.

New techniques were also being developed to increase tenure for stylists. The private label beauty product line now included their own and seven national brands sold throughout The Barbers locations and also to clients in six countries.

Much of the early financing for growth that was needed by members of Joe's original barbers, was provided by Joe himself. Many of these deals were held together by "bailing wire," not sophisticated legalese in lengthy documents. Many of the new millionaires would tell you there was no possible way they could have bought their own locations without Joe's dedication to helping them. His heart was filled with passion to make a poor man rich. No doubt, his childhood played a part. He had experienced extreme poverty and was determined to rise above it, taking many new franchisees with him. Because of this, he was very lenient with many of his franchisees when they got behind on their scheduled payments. All of them say today that they know Joe would just "glow" if he could see how well off they have become.

Early franchise owner and prior barber for Joe, Gil Gilbertson said in 2004: "My wife, Rosie and I grew our biggest salon from 1,200 square feet to 10,000 square feet. Today we have ninety employees in that salon and do over $5,000,000 annually. We've been rated in the Top 200 Salons nationwide by *Salon Today* magazine for the past 4 years." When he met Joe for the first time for an interview, he was impressed with Joe's Highland shop. He was a little apprehensive but Joe made him feel comfortable and he was hired. What he noticed was that all the guys were real team players and displayed no cockiness—they genuinely wanted to help a new man become a part of the team.

Gil would learn a great deal, rubbing elbows with Joe and listening to how Joe worked with his customers. He also accepted Joe's advice on real estate investing and went on to become one of the many "phenoms" in The Barbers Franchise system. He and Rosie were the first multiple unit owners in the system.

Bill Kaminski, early Franchise owner and former barber for Joe: "When Joe suggested I open my own salon, my greatest fear was being under-capitalized. But Joe helped me with the financing and it was the only way I could have gotten off the ground." He was broke and thought that he'd never get hired because of his background. "Joe helped me in many ways. The real estate thing was big and he also told me never to buy a new car. He said—always buy a two-year old Cadillac."

Through Joe's mentoring, Kaminski eventually owned dozens of real estate rental units, which helped, finance his salon expansion and solidify his success. In 2004, Kaminski owned over 80 salons.

As 1978 closed out, Joe felt it was their best year since the franchise start-up. They had 500 people in the organization, the balance sheet was improving and there were 47 franchises and 31 corporate salons in place. Income hit $5,774,477 and pre-tax income was up 94% over the prior year. He planned for aggressive growth in 1979. The company opened two new Barber schools, 21 new franchises and 5 more corporate salons that year. They celebrated their success and the company's Silver Anniversary (25 years) with a black tie event held at the Hotel Sofitel in Minneapolis. They also moved their headquarters to 300 Industrial Blvd. in Northeast Minneapolis; a major expansion for them.

Joe had found the building on Industrial Blvd. and really liked it; he contacted the seller to discuss the possibilities of a purchase. The owner, Frank Griswold, had run his coffee roasting and vending company from this location for many years. Frank had personally designed the elaborate interior. The two met and Joe told Frank his company was doing well but it didn't look good on paper. The Barbers, despite record income, had a poor earnings record, was heavily leveraged and Joe was very short on cash. Frank was impressed by Joe being so forthright. Joe gave Frank his banker's name and number and Frank called the banker.

A meeting was set up. The banker, Jim Reissner, had dealt with Joe for years. He saw Joe as a very honest, enthusiastic and trustworthy person. Joe thought buying the building was impossible because he had no down payment. Flo heard that Griswold was immensely proud of the unique beauty and quality of the property. She told Joe to 'go back and tell Griswold the building was the finest, most beautiful property in the city. If there was a way he could get a few months cost free, he would pay back with interest and never miss a payment, and most importantly, keep the building in pristine condition and never disturb the original design or decor.'

When they met, Joe followed through on Flo's advice and told Frank how much he admired the building (he sincerely did) and promised Frank he'd never have to worry about the payment. Frank said he'd think about it.

After Joe left the meeting, Jim and Frank discussed the deal. They talked about Joe's character, reputation and his sincere interest in maintaining the building. They both agreed on Joe's integrity and desire to succeed and they structured a financing plan. Joe gratefully accepted this plan and never missed nor was late on a single payment. Jim Reissner said in later years that Joe could get more out of a banking relationship than most men could, due to his charismatic personality and sincerity.

Joe also recruited a new member to his training team in '79 that he felt would become an important addition. At a competitor company, Horst Salons, was a stylist and trainer that caught Joe's attention. Joe had a successful stylist working with him named Mary Cole. Her husband, Michael, was the Artistic Director at Horst, and Joe liked him. In conversations Joe had with Mary, he arranged a dinner meeting with the two them.

Mary Cole was making more money working for Joe as a stylist than Michael was making in his key position with Horst. Joe told Michael he wanted him to join The Barbers and work first as a stylist and then as a trainer. However, Michael would have to subscribe to Joe's customer service philosophy, attend two full weeks of training (vs. the normal one week for new stylists) and consider a whole new approach to building a customer base. If Michael could handle it, Joe would pay him $30,000/year or commission, whichever was greater, a considerable increase in pay. Joe asked Michael how many different haircuts he knew. Michael thought—maybe fifty. Joe said, "If I watched you do fifty haircuts, I bet at most you're going to call on just five to ten of the fifty you know. And you'll do that every single day except for the occasional avant-garde client, where you'll pull one of your super-creative tricks out of your bag." Joe told him that 85% of his long-term financial success would come from *how he communicated* with clientele and associates and only 15% had to do with how he cut hair.

This was a revelation for Michael, who was an excellent stylist and proud of his work. Joe went on to say that clients can tell the difference between a good haircut and a bad one but that very few can recognize a technically perfect cut. On the other hand, all clients can tell when they're getting exceptional service—give them exceptional service and you'll build a large and strong clientele. Even though Joe felt that Michael was somewhat skeptical, he saw great potential in him and envisioned a positive future for both of them.

Michael Cole: "Joe told me The Barber's philosophy was different from Horst and the other salons. He asked me to give him six months and have blind faith in what I was shown and would learn. Joe said his intention was to serve my best interest and that if it didn't work in six months, I could go back to doing what I had been doing. He also told me he believed my life was going to explode and create a change in prosperity I couldn't even imagine.

I never had anyone talk to me at this depth before, so I made a decision that day. I would not make judgments about Joe or his ideas, nor argue with any of it. I was going to buy in."

Michael Cole later said that he learned more about the hair business than ever before. Joe sent him to many seminars that resulted in Michael becoming motivated to take on a key training and motivational speaking position. From this launch pad, Michael went on to develop the company's *Stylist Awareness Seminar* and *The Formula for Success Plan,* both based on Joe's customer service philosophy.

With the company growing, timing for Cole's arrival could not have been better. Joe Francis was traveling more for the International Franchise Association and the franchisees were seeing less of him. This created some well-founded concern among many of them. The older franchises were getting calls from the newer ones looking for help; calls that they thought should be directed to the home office. Michael's training helped to quell these concerns.

However, because Joe was so busy, there were still some worried franchisees. Dale Horsfield, from Iowa, teamed up with Bill Kaminski from Wisconsin and Ron Peterson from North Dakota. Together they organized a *Franchise Advisory Board*. These entities are common today but were rare in the 1970s, even with the best franchise companies. The Board was designed to provide franchisees with a voice regarding concerns, complaints, requests or suggestions directed to the Franchiser. Joe was wary of the concept, and probably felt a little betrayed by their actions, but Joe was losing contact with these people due to his hectic and demanding schedule. He knew the situation required some sort of "fix" but wasn't sure their approach was the answer. The three organizers wanted this Board to be a positive and supportive body that would enhance company growth. Flo would say later that Joe wondered why his loyal colleagues were concerned. The group was able to persuade Joe that it was in his best interest to have their feedback, and they weren't out to get him. They had a huge stake in the business and wanted to make sure everyone came out a winner. Their efforts paid off. The Franchise Advisory Board became a solid connection between the franchisees and the home office. The relationship proved to be positive and extremely helpful for company growth.

Joe kept encouraging Cole to fine tune the training and Michael came up with an idea for a huge, company-wide motivational rally he called *Super Sunday Seminar for Success*. It started with about 500 attendees and grew to over 700 stylists as a recurring yearly event. Joe was certainly proud of the progress Michael was making. After Cole had been with the company several years, he bought his own franchise—at Joe's suggestion. He was fully committed to the company now. Joe continually encouraged Michael to take more courses, classes and listen to tapes that would enhance his ability to lead and communicate. At one point, some classes Michael wanted to take at the University of Minnesota were graduate classes. He didn't have a degree and they refused to enroll him. Joe said, "Look, call up the professor; tell him who you are and what you're doing. Tell him you're our Director of Training." Michael followed through and was enrolled. The company paid for the classes and Joe enjoyed being part of the process that propelled Coles' success.

Time passed and Joe realized that Michael's real strengths were in his ability to train and motivate franchisees and The Barbers staff. Joe set up another meeting with him. This time he told Michael he thought he should sell his franchise and build his own motivational training company. Joe thought Michael's talent and skills could result in a bright future and even though Joe would lose him, he wanted Michael to enjoy all the success he could.

After much consideration, Michael did start his own company, *Salon Development Corporation*. All the time, effort and preparation that he had put in, at the advice of his mentor, paid off. He *doubled* his income his first year. But he couldn't see how he could do much more, as he only had so much time and was booked up. Joe suggested that he consider selling tapes and books like other successful speakers. Michael said he didn't have any idea how to do that but Joe told him to just go learn how. He knew Michael could do it. Michael followed through and over time developed a huge following in the industry and became the noted author of several books about how to be successful in the hair business: "A Little Off The Top," "Stop Getting By and Start Getting Rich" and "A Handbook for Exceptional Salon Profits." Many of his books have a thank you or dedication page to Joe. Michael's company is recognized today as a top training organization worldwide and continues successfully.

Declining earnings for The Barbers in 1979 followed the closing of one of their barber schools. Two corporate salons had closed the year before. However, the company declared a stock split dividend of two shares for each share of outstanding stock. Coming into 1980, the company's salons faced stiff competition in a then shaky market. The US economy was in trouble and headed into a recession. To further exacerbate matters, loans outstanding experienced rate increases from an already high 14 3/4% to 23%. Joe would say: *"It was difficult for me to separate emotions and private feelings from the cold, hard business decisions that had to be made. I can't tell you how tough it was for me. I had to let some good people go."* His dedicated administrative staff willingly took on an overload of work to help the company squeeze through during this period.

Many prospective franchisees had to abandon their decisions to buy or postpone their salon openings as banks tightened lending requirements. The company was forced to close three franchises that couldn't make payments on what they owed. The economy was in bad shape with a looming recession, which would turn out to be the worst since the Great Depression.

There was even more grief! 1979 was a particularly trying year for Joe Francis. The IRS brought to his attention that he could no longer hire or retain managers and stylists as independent contractors. The stylists and managers at that time were independent contractors, paying their own taxes and social security deposits. They worked on commission, without guarantees, and made substantially more money compared to other independent barbers. Now, all stylists and managers had to be employees. They were to be paid hourly or salaried and could no longer be independent contractors. As employees, the company would have to guarantee them a wage and pay into the employee's Social Security account. These were serious adjustments but they had to be made. Bob Vaa, then Executive Vice President and head of Tiro Industries, advised Joe to hold off on announcing this change until their accountant could give him all the information he needed to make a proper presentation. As usual though, Joe figured he could "wing it"; he set up a meeting and made the announcement. Not good!

Some stylists didn't believe it was an IRS ruling but must have thought it was a Joe Francis brain storm. Others understood the requirement but worried it would create a huge wage reduction. Chaos followed. The result was a 25% turnover in stylists. Charlie Brown called it "a revolt." This was when Peggy Schmidt, the stylist Joe had supported many times, jumped off the bandwagon and quit. She and Joe would always remain friends, however.

The years following this ruling continued to create hiring and retention problems. Jim Curran was Regional Manager of The Barbers' Harrisburg, Pennsylvania shops. Jim: "1981 was the worst year of my life. It created a commission-ectomy and many of the people, who had been with us for years, left us. We experienced a 100% turnover." The company eventually recovered; this was just another hurdle in a long line of hurdles.

A U.S. Franchise Trade mission was headed for Japan in 1980. Joe had met an enterprising and ambitious barber from Japan at the Centennial celebration and National Association of Barber Schools Convention in Washington D.C. in 1976. When they met, Joe shared his story and passion for franchising with him. His name is Takayoshi (Tak) Nomoto. When Joe decided to go with the 1980 Trade Mission, he wrote to Tak and told him he would be coming to Japan to find prospective Franchisees. The two men had really hit it off at their first meeting and Joe, who was always looking toward the future, was exploring the idea of putting franchises in Japan. Perhaps Tak would be interested; or at a minimum, connect Joe with other Japanese barbers.

Tak knew that Joe was pretty aggressive and he had concerns about how Joe would approach the market in Japan. There were obvious cultural differences. He wrote to Joe, expressing his concerns. He'd help Joe, by getting some audiences together for Joe to make presentations to, but he did have reservations. Joe wrote back, telling Tak he would not do anything to offend or embarrass Tak or his associates. When Joe and Flo arrived in Japan, they were received like royalty! Tak and his wife, Fusako, were the most gracious of hosts. Flo was intrigued with the Japanese kimono and Fusako helped her to don one in all its complexity. They all had a lovely time together at the Nomoto home.

Tak offered to interpret for Joe at a banquet he had set up. Joe was a hit with his Japanese audience. Tak had told him that only 20% of the salons in Japan were considered upscale or similar to The Barbers. When Joe took a tour of the local salons he was amazed! Japanese salon owners shared Joe's customer service philosophy and kept their skills honed through training. He couldn't see a market for his concept there because all the salons were extremely well managed, kept in immaculate condition and were thriving very efficiently. They also practiced excellent customer service. The trip was still considered a huge success though, as Joe and Flo would become intimate friends with the Nomoto family. The Francis' insisted that the Nomotos visit Minneapolis so that Joe and Flo could reciprocate their hospitality. A year later, the Nomotos arrived in Minneapolis. They enjoyed a gala reception and toured The Barbers headquarters and salons, and took in many of the Twin Cities cultural attractions. The families formed a bond that lives on today.

In 1981, while plodding through an ugly economy, now entrenched in a serious recession, The Barbers still managed to slowly grow. They invested over $100,000 in their training facilities. In his annual report that year, Joe said: "We didn't earn a profit but we invested in better training for our stylists. We'll not only benefit with increased sales but our stylists' income will increase, which is necessary to have a happy workforce." As an avid reader and self-taught entrepreneur, he had a deep-seated belief in continual training. He was convinced it forestalled many problems and resulted in longer employee tenure.

In later years, in a 1987 interview with Minnesota's *Corporate Report Magazine,* Joe Francis is quoted as saying: *"I had a hundred stores in 1982, doing between $6-$7 million in sales but I was in way over my head. I decided to look for a CEO and step back to assume the role of Chairman of The Board."* It took courage to recognize his own lack of formal business credentials. There was every chance he would have to make adjustments in the process, but Joe was a visionary and he didn't like the vision he was getting. Even a lumberjack steps back to sharpen his axe now and then and Joe was stepping back to evaluate, so he could march ahead again.

Reaching for a solution to increase traffic flow through the salons, Tom Tweed, The Barbers Marketing Director, aimed their advertising efforts in a new direction. Tom had discovered through considerable research, that a large segment of the population was opposed to the upscale prices at The Barbers salons. He found that their average ticket of $19.25 wasn't going to draw in the average customer on the street. He also learned that 50% of their customers were women. Something had to change.

CHAPTER 7

COST CUTTERS

In the summer of 1982, Joe received a call from a Canadian company that was marketing a value-priced hair salon franchise concept. They wanted to know if The Barbers cared to consider being the Master Franchiser for the USA. Joe wasn't very interested but his business sense made him think he should check out this possible competitor. Joe sent his Operations Manager to Canada on a due diligence trip.

His manager came back and recommended The Barbers start something similar, a quick hair cut for a cheap price, aiming at high-traffic locations and catering to the masses. Joe didn't want to go back to a simple haircut process. By this time The Barbers were revolutionizing the industry and their managers and stylists took great pride in their skills and upscale styling accomplishments. Joe sent his manager back to Canada again, telling him to learn all he could about how this company was operating. When his manager returned, he told Joe: "Listen, Joe, we gotta do this. It's a good program, they're coming to the States and we gotta beat them to the punch."

But Joe was adamant! He was not going to go backwards—no value-priced haircutting for him. His Operations Manager actually threatened to do it on his own and compete with The Barbers, which is exactly what he did.

Later that year, Joe called an emergency meeting of his faithful management team. They met on the patio at his lake home. Joe began: "Well, the operations manager I let go did decide to come into this area with the value-priced-haircut concept. I need to know from you guys what we should do—should we get into this too, with our own concept, or just stay with what we're doing?"

Once again, Earl Faulkner was the first to speak. Earl said "Joe, I believe we've needed this for a long time and I for one support it. If you want to do this, I'll throw in with you. In fact, if you want to franchise that chain, I'll buy your first franchise." Joe went from man to man, querying everyone for their thoughts but no one, other than Earl, stood for or against the idea. Joe thought for a few moments then said, "Well, OK, that's it. We're going to do it."

Off and running again! Joe now asked Flo about this new value-priced idea, what should they call it? What would be a good name? They brainstormed, wrote out a list of possibilities which Joe took to the office the next day to run by his staff. That evening he came home and announced to Flo "It's done. We're going to call it "Budget Hair." Flo couldn't believe her ears, "That sounds degrading Joe—sounds like a cheap, second-class operation. It doesn't reflect who and what you are. You want a name that projects the right image!" Joe said, "Well, it's already done—that's what we decided." Flo said he'd have to *undo* it then. "That name is terrible she said, it has to go!" What followed was one of their most memorable arguments. Flo said years later: "I was just as mad as he was, there was no way this was going to stand. We battled for hours!" The next morning, Joe went into the office with Flo's replacement name. They'd call the new business "*Cost Cutters*."

Earl Faulkner remembers Joe calling him to tell him the new value-priced chain of the franchise would be called "*Cost Cutters*." Earl: "It struck me as perfect and I wasn't surprised that Flo came up with it. She was a helluva behind-the-scenes person. Whatever inspiration we got from Joe through his belief system, he must've got the same thing from Flo through her support system."

Cost Cutters was born. A whole new concept that would challenge beliefs, tap everyone's energy, create unseen problems and opportunities but enormously increase revenues. They had learned that the industry had various price strata that served a diverse customer base. Customers looking for hair styling wouldn't care to be in a salon that also catered to children. On the other hand, customers, especially families in hurry or those just looking for fast service and an inexpensive cut, weren't looking for a styling salon. This new concept brought in less per customer, but it increased volume immensely.

One major problem emerged regarding the sometimes close proximity of one "Cost Cutters" shop to locations of other Cost Cutters. The customer for Cost Cutters took the first available stylist because they wanted to get in and out quickly and pay less. They didn't identify with the stylist, the way customers who patronized the upscale salons did. Consequently, they didn't care so much *who* cut their hair, just that it was fast and economical. As they drove down the road, they'd tend to pull into the first "Cost Cutters" they saw. This created a problem because the franchisees wanted larger boundary lines. The company quickly realized they needed to establish development boundaries for each location, to avoid encroachment problems.

The Barbers marketing department developed the Cost Cutters concept to clearly be perceived as an alternative to the upper-end Barbers Salons. The new look of Cost Cutters was clean, bright, colorful and inexpensive. These shops didn't require upscale locations. Families on tight budgets, school-age youngsters, and blue collar workers were comfortable walking into less glitzy, retail strip center surroundings. This made it easier to find locations and there were more to choose from. Another benefit to opening a Cost Cutters franchise was the lower investment for the franchise start-up and operating costs. This meant there was a larger segment of the investing public from which to draw. Business started to boom!

Joe wanted to have several impressive, operating model salons for prospective franchisees to visit, while they were in the decision-making process. He decided to convert some of the existing Barbers Salons, those in the lower income areas where the more expensive razor cut was not doing so well, into model Cost Cutters Salons. As usual, his backup team kicked in and started helping with the conversion by painting and changing the decor. Within a week, two of Joe's own original five salons were transformed into company-owned "Cost Cutters," and two new locations were opened at the same time. A quick haircut was just $6.00.

Marketing Director, Tom Tweed: "The shops were painted red and yellow, which sent a message of family-friendly and economical." They also developed and ran TV commercials aimed at families and a younger audience. In September, 1982, they had a whole new concept in place, just weeks after making the decision to go ahead. When Joe was ready to do something, he got it done. Joe contacted a local TV station with news about the discount haircut concept. The TV station sent out a reporter to cover the story at one of the transformed salons. Joe expounded on the virtues of the $6.00 haircut, moving from one end of the shop to the other, followed by the cameras. It was another successful publicity piece and made the grand opening a resounding success.

When the "Cost Cutters" franchise offering was finally approved, Earl Faulkner put his money on the table. He opened just north of downtown Minneapolis and said "the shop went like gang busters!" By opening at this lightning clip, Cost Cutters was the first value-priced salon chain to open in the Twin Cities market, ahead of the efforts of Joe's previous manager and the Canadian company that first posed a threat. Always competitive, always good in business foresight—Joe got there first!

The new concept wasn't designed to replace the company's upscale salons. Some thought Joe was going back to his one-man shop days and simple haircuts. Not so, he was adding to the menu, just like franchise industry giant, McDonalds. Loyal to their classy Barbers Salons, many of his Founders Team stayed their distance for awhile—not ready to go this route. Once they understood that serving these two, very different customer bases could only enhance and increase their opportunity to expand, they got in the game and many got in deep! The company-measured customer crossover rate, from salons to Cost Cutters, was just 8% the first year. There was really nothing to fear.

Joe realized he'd made some early corporate management mistakes in his selection of advisory and marketing people. Many of his loyal staff agreed. On the other hand, his selection of barbers was superb. Visionaries like Joe, are in the race to win; so they jump in the chariot, whack the horse with a whip and take off. But now, Joe, sharpening his focus, saw the need to hire seasoned, degreed professionals, and delegate to them in the areas of their expertise. The result was a huge increase in operational effectiveness, which led to more franchise openings and the support that they needed.

Joey, the first-born son of Joe and Flo Francis, had been around the business doing a variety of tasks ever since he was just a little boy. He had been involved in everything from cleaning to painting and product delivery. When he was 12 years old, he also worked as a shoeshine boy in Joe's salons. Now he was assigned to working with the company franchisees. He had graduated from St. Thomas College with a Business and Marketing degree, which he used to fine-tune the franchise's needs. In 1984, Joey took over management of three of Joe's personally-owned salons. His experience there gave him the confidence to open his own "Cost Cutters" franchise in 1985. Shortly thereafter, he and Joe went to the bank for a $100,000 loan so Joey could build-out three more "Cost Cutters" locations in the Twin Cities. John Francis, Joey's younger brother said "Joey's Grand Avenue location was a knockout and his Roseville location was great too!"

Joey eventually owned six "Cost Cutters" salons and one original Barbers salon. He was busy growing his Twin Cities franchises, doing all the accounting, managing, inventory, payroll taxes and employee meetings. He didn't know it then but his dad would increase his work load later down the road.

In an industrial city, like Dubuque, Iowa, where at that time, unemployment at local plants is in a runaway mode, an upscale styling salon will suffer for it. Dale Horsfield, a salon owner in Dubuque: "It was a tough period for higher priced salons. I bought into the "Cost Cutters" concept—felt the $6.00 cut was what we needed. I had to work to calm the fears of my staff but sure enough, within a month, my "Cost Cutters" began to soar in Dubuque."

Walt Freiberg operated two Barbers salons in western Minnesota and was about as busy as he wanted to be. He said that "silver-tongued" Joe convinced him to open a "Cost Cutters." He agreed and on his first day of business, he had people lined-up outside his door. The fence sitters started buying in. "Cost Cutters" really began to sail and have a big impact on the company's bottom line.

One early holdout, Bill Kaminski, recognized a superior advantage the Cost Cutters concept had over the upscale salons. He said he was tired of being held hostage by stylists who, if they left, took their clientele with them. With "Cost Cutters," the customer wasn't as concerned about who cut their hair. If a stylist left, the clientele stayed—they were loyal to the location, not the stylist. Kaminski built five "Cost Cutters" locations in Madison, WI in just six months. By 1996, this aggressive hard-working entrepreneur, who originally thought Joe would never hire him, owned forty six "Cost Cutters" in three states. Bill Kaminski was an exemplary franchisee for The Barbers organization. And who could have predicted that the "Cost Cutters" growth would outstrip the company's other salon growth by 10 times within four years of inception?

By 1986, staunch supporter, former manager and salon owner, Dale Loucks, joined the parade. He opened his first "Cost Cutters" salon right next to his Forest Lake, MN upscale Barbers salon. It was an instant success.

In 1982, during this exciting but challenging period of growth, Joe was still searching for help at the top. He realized his value to the company was in his visionary leadership not in management. The company hired a consulting firm, which recommended they interview a candidate named Mike Jorgensen. Like Joe, he had an entrepreneurial core and the two hit it off. He was hired to come on as a consultant. Joe was also working on a personal problem that year. He hadn't been feeling well for sometime and had scheduled a physical exam. No one was ready for the grave diagnosis—he had cancer. His doctors insisted they operate soon and told him this would be very aggressive surgery; he'd be out of action for some time. Within a week, Joe was at the Mayo Clinic in Rochester, Minnesota for surgery.

Searching for a new accounting candidate, Jorgensen phoned Joe in the hospital to talk with him about a prospect he had in mind. Joe had him come down to the clinic the night before his operation to discuss the new hire. After their meeting, he told Jorgensen to hire the man. When he recovered from his operation, Joe came into headquarters for a meeting with Jorgensen. Knowing he was facing a lengthy recovery period, he needed someone else to take over as CEO. Jorgensen seemed to be doing a good job at this point so Joe asked him to become their CEO. Jorgensen accepted the position. The company had also hired new legal counsel, Tom McIntosh, who was an experienced and successful local franchise attorney.

Joe preferred early morning breakfast meetings, often saying the day is half gone by 6:30 a.m. Being an avid reader, Joe probably had read and subscribed to Benjamin Franklin's opinion, "early morning hath gold in its mouth." At one of these early morning meetings in 1983, Joe told McIntosh, "We've been doing things wrong. We should sell multiple franchises to our existing franchisees because *they* are proven operators." Starting in 1984, The Barbers began what would be an explosive and positive move, the selling of multiple units—entire franchise areas they called "Development Agreements." Joe felt this would be superior to the one to two salon approach they had taken before. They looked for investors who had pockets deep enough to buy up to ten salons. For existing franchisees, the "Cost Cutters" concept was quicker and easier to set up and manage compared to their upscale units. Counsel McIntosh said "It put the company over the top."

These multi-unit deals brought in bigger-thinking investors who brought with them serious investment dollars. That year the company also landed a national contract to sell the premiere line of hair care products, The "Paul Mitchell" line. Along with their own private label line through Tiro Industries, they had an impressive and extensive product line. Their product sales were up by 22.6% in 1984. But, the best news that year was: Joe had his cancer in remission.

The company ended 1984 with 60 "Cost Cutters" in eight states, 123 of "The Barbers" Salons in thirteen states (all both corporate and franchisee owned), and six barber schools in five states. Sales soared to over $10,000,000.

Gaining momentum, the company forged ahead with impressive gains in 1985. They had a total of 256 salons, up from 183 of the previous year. Sales were up to $12.8 million, pushing net income to $162,000. Joe's strategic move to integrate the "Cost Cutters" concept was responsible for most of this growth. That division of the company comprised 141 salons, in just a few years from inception. Joe wrote in the Annual Report: "we expect to double these numbers in 1986."

It was time for more private-label hair products for the Cost Cutters salons. New packaging and product development meant the customer could choose from three different shampoos, two conditioners, control mist, setting gel, clarifier, a vitamin treatment and mousse. Joe wanted the company to lead the industry with the most complete and high-quality line of products available. They had learned their lesson years ago, product sales were critical to maintaining a healthy bottom line. This meant greater profits for franchisees, which helped sell new franchises and which translated into a big win for the company.

As the pace was picking up in the mid 1980s, John Francis, (Joe's youngest son), while a student at St. Thomas College, had been working at The Barbers headquarters and helped his older brother Joey as well. During a meeting in father Joe's office, he couldn't help but notice unorganized file cabinets full of real estate leases, invoices and other matters pertaining to properties Joe owned. As he started looking through the mess, he found that some of Joe's tenants had not been paying rent. In John's words, "It was a train wreck." He approached his dad. "Would you mind if I organized your real estate business for you?" Joe was more than happy with the idea. He told John to just take it over—organize and manage it. John, not long past his 19th birthday, dug right in.

He handled everything from building maintenance and repair to collecting rents, evicting tenants who didn't pay, and filling vacancies. Joe had been a soft touch for too many tenants, he loved to help people when they were down but many of these people took advantage of his kind heart. John, a full time college student, managed the properties while he was still providing maintenance support for the family owned franchise salons, and also working with his brother, Joey.

This regimen continued for three years before John turned over the real estate business, now established as *Francis Development Company,* to John Low, an acquaintance of his dad. Joe and Low were working on a strip mall project together and Joe had confidence in Low's ability. John Francis had been responsible for 14 properties, 32 tenants and the bookkeeping for a $600,000 rent roll.

Another important event took place in 1985. Joe's former attorney, Howard Stacker, who had joined the Board of Directors, resigned from his position. With a business partner, he purchased the multi-salon franchise rights for "Cost Cutters" in Colorado. Their aggressive plan was to open eighteen salons in 14 months. During the planning and development stage, they found this initial forecast was inadequate for that market. They really needed to open thirty salons to support their goals and that would require a huge additional investment they didn't have.

Howard approached Joe and then CEO, Mike Jorgensen. Stacker wanted the company to buy back his multi-salon rights along with the salons they had already opened. Joe took his considerable negotiating skills and ever-present charisma to his banker. He came back with $1 million and bailed out Stacker. Although Jorgenson thought this to be a damaging move, in later years, it would prove to be a good decision on Joe's part.

Joe was having a busy year. Now, as he turned the corner, here came a freight train right at him. The U.S. Bank Corporation was unhappy with one of the company loans, a $3 million loan. It's a very serious situation when your bank tells you to pay off a loan and you don't have the money to do it with. But Joe is not afraid. He does have to come up with a game plan though, this one won't be easy. The $3 million note was *unsecured,* given on Joe's personal guarantee. Now that in itself was a monumental move Joe had already pulled off! How in the world he convinced the bank to make that loan, one could only guess. There was enough pressure on Joe from day to day with all the company growth and management problems, now this?

Because the growth forecast projected by the company had not been met, the bank put the company on a "work out," a method to make correction to perform as projected. This resulted in micro-monitoring by the bank. The company's financial advisor, Richard King, had a talk with Joe. He wanted Joe to be careful about his projections and promises, the company *had* to deliver. Joe told Richard, "Well, you've got to schmooze these people." Richard told Joe, "I've been in the financial business all my life and the last people you want to schmooze are bankers. If you don't produce, they get concerned." Since Joe was the one who schmoozed them to get the $3 million note in the first place, he didn't think this was any serious problem.

At that time, many corporations inflated their reports to lenders—but Joe never did. As the bank continued to monitor its investment, they called Joe in to review the whole situation. Throughout the entire Metro area, the bank was putting pressure on companies that were behind on payments and performance. Joe went to another bank, the Norwest Bank, and told them what US bank was doing. Norwest Bank could see the company supporting a $1.6 million loan, but not $3 million, and certainly, not an unsecured loan. Board member, David Emerson, said: "Joe went to Norwest Bank, put up all his personal assets and negotiated a $1.6 million loan. Had he not done that, the company would not have survived."

Now everything Joe owned was on the line. No one person in a public corporation ever sticks their neck out like this. Joe went back to US Bank and offered them $1.6 million to write off the $3 million loan. US Bank went for it. As far as Joe was concerned, the company had just made $1.4 million.

For Joe, change usually came easy. However, in 1986, The company was looking to update and revamp many of The Barbers' original upscale salons. They were also considering a name and logo change. They hired an advertising firm to come in and conduct some brainstorm sessions. During the first session, Joe was visibly upset and walked out of the meeting. After all, this company and brand was his baby and choosing a new name was hard to accept. He cooled off though, came back in and they resumed. They decided on a new logo and changed the company's upscale salon name from The Barbers to "City Looks." With this, Joe had to face the arduous task of informing and selling all the salon owners on this new look and name. This update and name change would mean an expense of about $6,000 to $14,000 per location. There was much concern about how this change would be received by the older salon owners.

Fortunately, some of these original owners; Gil & Rosy Gilbertson, Don and Deborah Thorpe; Gary Clausen; Earl Faulkner, all leaders amongst The Barbers franchisees, embraced the change to "City Looks" and led the field. (The parent company name, however, remained "The Barbers.")

It turned out well. By the end of 1987, sales in these revamped salons were up 20% and their cosmetic sales grew by 30%. The media helped bolster the company's credibility and growth in 1986 as well. The Barbers were ranked as the *sixth fastest-growing franchiser* by Venture Magazine. Joe wrote a memo to all his associates and franchisees, "I can't help but think about our next twenty five years. It's amazing when I look back at 1963 and try to remember what I was thinking when Flo and I put the idea of The Barbers together. We really had no plan at that time to be a multi-chain company. I can honestly say and finally give public recognition to Flo, my wife, who was instrumental in causing me to reach beyond my own capabilities, to step up two social classes higher than I ever hoped to be. It was Flo who gave me input and ideas of what our new salon concept was to be."

He went on to say that after traveling the world and getting to know the leaders in the hair industry, he was convinced that The Barbers had the best people, program and systems to lead the industry in the next 25 years. Joe encouraged them to be willing to embrace change when the timing was right. He also forecasted that the 1990s would see more women in business and this would require more flexible hours for stylists. The future would include more women and minorities chasing the American dream through franchise ownership.

At the company convention in 1987, Joe wanted to recognize the dedication and loyalty a very important person provided to the company. It's one thing to perform at a meritorious level if one is paid well for it. However, Flo Francis was performing for the company at many different levels, persevering through the various Joe Francis maneuvers; she was doing it all for him and she had never gotten a paycheck. Joe realized how fortunate he was and in 1987 he initiated and awarded Flo the company's "Behind the Scenes Award." (It later became the "Flo Francis Award.") Flo, was honored for the time, effort, creative work and public relations she was doing for the company and for taking on the jobs of Social Director and Newsletter Editor. This award became a coveted recognition among the Founder's Club wives and franchise owners as well.

The Flo Francis awards reads:

With every successful enterprise, there are people behind the scenes who have put in measureless energy and effort and who have made an unselfish commitment to work with, sacrifice, and support the person, generally the public figure and the one given the credit for the enterprise's success.

This person is rarely on the payroll, never gets much credit for their input and, in most cases, has made very significant contributions. Sometimes this has been to the expense of their own career and growth and has much to do with the tremendous responsibility of raising the

> *family of the entrepreneur who is away from home a great deal of the time attempting to become successful.*
>
> *Success could never be achieved without this behind-the-scenes person's sacrifice. Our company, employees, and franchisees truly appreciate your efforts.*

From the reaction of all present, they did agree and gave Flo Francis a much deserved, standing ovation.

Joe now foresaw the inability of many independent salons being able to compete. He foretold; they'd be dominated by strong chains and franchises in the industry. He cautioned these independent salons to watch for a shake-out in the business, where smaller, weaker chains and franchisers would succumb to and be bought out by the more dominant ones.

His vision was prophetic. In fact, The Barbers would be one of those players who in later years would be buying out these less-successful chains and franchises. He knew too, that in order to attract the best and most talented stylists, barbers and managers, the company would have to build-in opportunity to facilitate growth, personal ownership and happy employees.

This was accomplished through training, flexible hours and benefits for the stylists. Joe encouraged salon ownership and family involvement, just as his own family had experienced. He said, "You and I have invested our lives in this business. If we continue to work together supporting each other, our future success will be secure. Our efforts will pay dividends not only to us but to our children and their children."

Joe Francis had another problem though, the cancer was back. He was facing more surgery and pain. Once again, his positive belief system kicked in, he believed he could beat it!

In the following year, the company learned about a Wal-Mart pilot project called Hyper-mart USA. This concept would add other services to the Wal-Mart retailing menu. Wal-Mart wanted to add a bank branch office, grocery section, photo studio, optometrist, food court, arcade and hair salon, all incorporated under one very large roof. About ten hair salon chains jumped into the bidding pool. Then CEO, Mike Jorgensen, pursued the opportunity and was successful. This was a monumental move, the company not only gained an opportunity for new Wal-Mart high-traffic locations, but also media coverage which contributed to the sale of new "Cost Cutters" franchises. Jorgensen headed for the first Grand Opening at Garland, Texas on December 28, 1987. While there, he met Sam Walton himself and showed Sam the "Cost Cutters" salon and was able to enlighten him on the philosophy. "Cost Cutters" was a perfect fit for the retailer's approach to serving the masses with value. Jorgensen was also successful in negotiating a contract for the next test location in Topeka, Kansas. It was a major move and brought with it outstanding publicity. On the march again! The Barbers opened Cost Cutter Salons in four more cities with Hyper-mart USA.

This relationship seemed to offer huge potential. Unfortunately, not long after this, Wal-Mart wasn't happy with their total project. They decided it needed refinement and put the project on hold. This resulted in The Barbers having to pull their "Cost Cutters" salons out of Wal-Mart locations and sell them as individual franchises. They accomplished this in short order and went on with their expansion plans. The relationship with Wal-Mart was still an opportunity they would continue to pursue.

Visionaries, like Joe Francis, are always thinking ahead, looking for new opportunities or for ways to improve what they have already created. This same year, Joe lead The Barbers in a strategic shift. Their growth plan would focus on building the franchise base vs. corporate salons. They decided to convert most of their company stores to franchises. Joe decided that he would buy the 20 company-owned salons in Pennsylvania and would be the franchise owner of these units. He borrowed the money from The Barbers and leveraged the real estate he personally owned in Francis Development. His loan would be a company asset. By doing this, he increased the company's income when he paid them for the salons. Board member David Emerson said: "The money was used to pay off *bank* debt and strengthen the bottom line; this enabled us to keep operating."

Flo remembers it well. She asked Joe why he would buy salons he already owned, as a majority stockholder? Joe told her this move would show more company income for the year. Flo was in a quandary over the matter. The 20 salons were over a thousand miles away, how would they be managed? Joe was already deeply in debt. His personal assets were on the line for the $1.6 million loan. He also had co-signed on a $100,000 note he and son Joey had signed when Joey opened three more Cost Cutters back in 1984. Yet, these financial obligations didn't slow him down. He went through with the purchase and the Francis family now owned 27 franchise salons. He called his sons Joey and John and said "I just bought 20 more salons and I need you guys to run these stores." The boys looked at each other and shook their heads, thinking "OK, Dad, whatever you want."

Things were moving at a rapid and furious clip. 1987 ended with sales over $17 million (up from $12.8 million in 1985). The company now had over 3,000 employees in 320 salons and 60 people on staff in the home office. "Cost Cutters" alone had created over 600 new jobs for Minnesotans, while growing to nearly 300 salons. More than 200 people had become successful franchise owners. Joe's penchant—to make a poor man rich—had already come to fruition. Many of his early, loyal followers were now millionaires. Some, like Joe, had come from disadvantaged or poor families. Thanks to Joe, two of these millionaires had been hired in their late teens, right out of a correction facility, a Reformatory. Joe saw something in them that others didn't. His keen intuition was the beginning of a successful transformation for these two men.

The 300th "Cost Cutters" salon opened in Sheboygan, Wisconsin in 1988. Jamil and Kitty Alaily, who won Franchisee of The Year, opened this salon, thereby adding to the eight they already owned. Their success was recognized and hyped by various accredited media, from newspapers to radio to TV. The Cost Cutters growth was phenomenal and Joe's goal was to open 700 more. Joe also wanted to continue the growth of the upscale, City Looks salons and the company was trying to find a way to lower the initial expense required to open them.

Jim George was the Director of Marketing for "Cost Cutters," and involved with the expansion program. He stepped up the salon advertising campaigns and was successful at gaining brand recognition.

Through this growth, turmoil and new daily challenges, Joe was battling cancer by following a strict, therapeutic diet regime, which included consuming organic juices hourly! The diet was so strict and complex that no restaurants had what he needed to eat. He bought a motor home that enabled him to keep up with his busy schedule while complying with his diet. The motor home was equipped with fax, phone, typewriter and a "juicer" for his exotic and hardly palatable diet. It had a full kitchen and he had his own cook in order to adhere to his diet regime. There was no holding Joe Francis back, the man would never quit fighting this disease. What a lot of people didn't know was that Joe, post surgeries, often worked from his hospital bed. How many people could, or even would, try to conduct their business from a hospital bed following major surgery? Joe insisted on having a phone at hand and the means to conduct business from his hospital room. It was a major driving force for him personally.

The company's 'Silver Anniversary' also took place in 1988. It was a time for great celebration, but the economy was not doing well and the company was mired in debt. Sales were good but the cost to manage company growth and services was outstripping income. The real estate market was bottoming out as well. Add to this, Joe's health prognosis, and things were not good. Joe had already gone through a great many grueling surgeries and now the doctors had begun the countdown. They didn't offer him much encouragement. This created an uncomfortable stir from the company staff and Board of Directors to the franchisees. If Joe passed on, what next? As far as the doctor's prognosis, Joe, as always, continued to be optimistic. He knew he was in a serious fight to regain his health, but he also knew he had to plan for the worst. Joe was passionate about getting the company on NASDAQ, a slow, detail-laden process but strategically a gargantuan move, if they could do it. Although Joe was very sick, he soldiered on.

He had worked with Flo and other team members, to build an impressive Board of Directors and management team with experience and talent. If things went bad for him, he wanted Flo to have strong backup support. Flo felt compelled to join the Board as Vice Chair, for continuity planning while Joe's stamina was waning. She wanted to be a voice for Joe when he couldn't be there. She also served on the company's Compensation Committee.

The 1988 Board of Directors included:

George Heenan, whose background included CEO of Medilase, Inc., Executive positions with Medical

Wellness Technologies, Inc., Medical Innovation Capital, Inc., Control Data, Medtronics, Inc. and Board of Governors of the University of Minnesota.

Richard King, Senior Financial Consultant with Swenson Halker, Inc., had served on the Board of Governors of Methodist Hospital and Lifespan, had been a Vice President for The Barbers, and was Vice President of Finance for International Multifoods Corporation and was past Vice President of Corporate Planning for SCM and the Glidden Co.

Rajiv Tanden, Professor in the Business Department at The College of St. Thomas, teaching entrepreneurship, served as a Consultant in Strategic Planning and New Venture Creation, was past Corporate Vice President and GM with National Car Rental System, Inc.

Fred Huggins, Vice President in the fast food and restaurant division of International Multifoods Corporation and President of its subsidiary, Mister Donut of America, Inc. Fred had a background of 23 years in franchising.

David Emerson, Dean of Accounting at The College of St. Catherine, St. Paul. He was introduced to the company by Flo, and was a consultant to the company prior to his appointment to the Board. Flo had taken several classes from David on interpreting P&L statements, balance sheets and other corporate financial management principals.

The Board was now steeped in talent and business management expertise. Having a powerful Board of Directors was a prerequisite to getting on NASDAQ.

This would be a more proactive Board. They suggested and agreed that all major management changes had to be run by and approved by them. Most entrepreneurs have difficulty with control measures like this but Joe reluctantly went along with their decision.

Another requirement for public companies, in order to get on NASDAQ, is to conduct annual audits by accredited financial organizations. The Barbers chose Ernst & Young as their auditors. David Emerson and the other members of the Board also decided it was time to replace the acting CEO. They needed a seasoned corporate executive, with franchise expertise for this position. While Jorgensen's contributions were appreciated, they felt he didn't have the business credentials necessary to carry the company forward. The Board members participated in the decision to hire the replacement for Jorgenson. But, in short order, Joe went ahead on his own and hired a candidate without consulting the Board.

This was a mistake that Joe himself began to realize and within a year, he let the man go. Joe's mistake was compounded by an employment contract he had signed with the dismissed CEO. Fred Huggins and the Board members informed Joe that there was not enough money to pay another CEO, because the one Joe let go had to be paid out of his contract. To correct things, Joe told them he'd come back as CEO and run the company. Everyone knew the job was way past Joe. There was no way he could do this, even if he was healthy. The company didn't need an entrepreneur; it needed a business degreed, franchise professional.

Prior to this event, the Franchise Advisory Board had set up a meeting with Huggins. They were very concerned about their investments and the future if Joe was gone. They came to Joe, Flo and the Board with their concerns. Flo remembers the meeting being painful for everyone. She was concerned for Joe, worrying that he would be hurt by the very same men he had supported for so long. They all loved Joe but rumors were that he didn't have much time left. They wanted to know how the company would survive his passing. Huggins was able to allay their fears, assuring them that the Board of Directors had a firm grip on taking the company forward.

The company grew steadily, thanks to Joe's vision and passion, but now, someone else would have to lead. Hard for Joe to accept; not only had he given the company all he had and risked every asset in his possession, he had performed through pain and misery, fighting a terminal disease all the way. But, more than anything, Joe wanted the company to grow and prosper. He loosened his grip on the throttle and took faith that his wife, family and staff would make good decisions. David Emerson said, "There was something spiritual about Joe—his drive, his focus, his personality. He really cared about people. He wanted to be successful so others would be too."

CHAPTER 8

GIVING BACK

One of the amazing things about Joe Francis was his ability to cope with surgeries and sickness while multi-tasking at The Barbers. He was also heavily involved in community and other projects to help people pursue *their* dreams. Joe believed he had an obligation to be *giving back* to the community, in which he had built the company.

In the early 1980s, a local entrepreneur, Norm Stoehr, started a business mentoring program for business owners to share ideas, experiences and methods they could all benefit from. Norm organized this program for small business and Joe became one of the mentors. Joe and Norm were proponents of networking and knew it would benefit these business owners. They connected personally and thoroughly enjoyed helping members grow their businesses. Initially, they tried a large group format. But after several years it evolved to smaller groups with similarities, which became a successful business venture for them.

Joe and Norm found they had a lot in common. They both came from the modus operandi of "ready, fire, aim." A partnership was formed. Joe proposed that they both sign with a bank for the start-up money and Norm would run it. Joe would help as he could. They called the new business "The Entrepreneur's Network." Norm found Joe to be a phenomenal partner; someone who always had time for him. This business later evolved to become "The Inner Circle" which is offered as a Business Format franchise today. Norm credits Joe for his mentoring and enthusiastic support through their years of association and very close friendship.

Joe was serving on the IFA (International Franchise Association) as a member of the Education Committee in 1990 and met Cheryl Babcock, the Executive Director at the International Center for Franchise Studies at the University of Nebraska. Joe thought the University of St. Thomas in St. Paul, Minnesota could offer a similar program. Both of his sons, Joey and John, had graduated from St. Thomas and Joe was impressed with the school. After several meetings with Cheryl, Joe, through The Barbers, pledged and donated $25,000 to St. Thomas to get a franchising course started and recommended Cheryl for the job. She had the right business background and had not only taught at the university level, she had owned a "Subway" franchise as well. Cheryl was an ambitious single mom with two children.

Joe was drawn to people who had a strong work ethic and were willing to take risks. She was hired for the job by St. Thomas. Arriving in St. Paul, Cheryl and her two children were greeted by Joe at the airport, and given a Twin Cities tour. Babcock said she had always been intimidated by successful people from big cities but Joe made her feel comfortable from their very first meeting.

She dug right in to her position and formed an Advisory Board, asking Joe to serve on it. He accepted and helped her recruit other members. Over the years, Cheryl developed an impressive curriculum that included five MBA franchise courses at St. Thomas.

She found Joe to be there for her throughout the formative process and a willing participant for her classes and seminars. Students gravitated to Joe and he was willing to share his mistakes with them as well as his successes. He offered The Barbers' headquarters for class field trips, so students could experience a real working, corporate model. Joe had a standing invitation for Cheryl, to fully utilize his franchise headquarters. She brought in people from England, Australia, Russia and Siberia. What Cheryl found amazing was that Joe was always accommodating. While she tried to be gracious about making appointments to bring in visitors, Joe would always say, "what days do you want to come out, just tell me how we can help." And, Joe and his staff would often stay late to help Cheryl when there were conflicting schedules. She was always impressed with the way Joe would greet her and her students during a visit to The Barbers facility. He would greet them with Flo and would say "this is my wife Flo, and she's the one that came up with the Cost Cutters name. She's also the one that puts a lot of systems in place for our franchisees and helps maintain that relationship." Cheryl found Joe to be very self-effacing and always giving credit to those he worked with.

Through the years, Joe took active and often key roles in many social, civic and business organizations. He was a Boy Scout Cub Master, active in his church—St. John's in Little Canada, MN. He also supported many charities, was Director for the National Association of Barber Schools, was past Vice President of Minnesota Associated Master Barbers, a member of St. Paul and Minneapolis Chambers of Commerce, Kiwanis Club of Minneapolis, St. Paul Winter Carnival Association, Highland Park Civic Association; Board of Directors of Mendota Hts., Jaycees; Minneapolis Housing and Redevelopment Committee, Minneapolis Small Business Council, International Council of Shopping Centers, Sales and Marketing Executives International, American Management Association. He had supported Missions and the children of West Africa, and the company held annual fundraisers for Children's Miracle Network and other causes for years. He supported The Jerry Lewis Telethon, The Danny Thomas Hospital Drive and The American Lung Association. Joe Francis was in perpetual motion.

The young couple, Joe and Flo, 1950.

Wedding day, April 23, 1955.

High school grad Joe Francis, 1953.

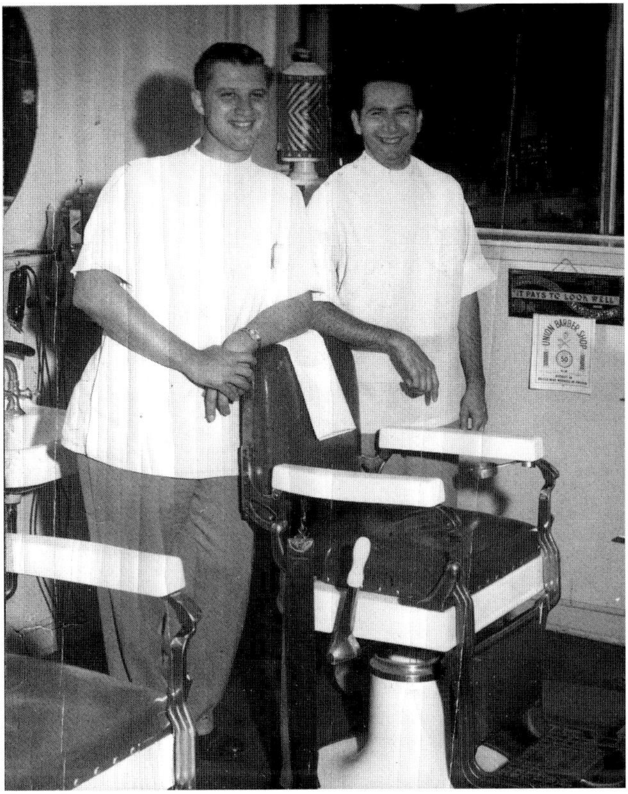

Joe with his first hire, Roy Oakes, 1961, on South Robert Street, in West St. Paul.

Ad from Suburban Life Magazine, Wednesday, March 22, 1961.

Grand opening of his upscale, Razor Cut and Styling Salon, 1963, in Highland Park, St. Paul.

These securities having been sold, this announcement appears only as a matter of record.

NEW ISSUE

100,000 Shares

Common Stock

(Par Value $.10 per share)

THE BARBERS, HAIRSTYLING FOR MEN, INC.

Price: $3.00 per share

Copies of the Offering Circular may be obtained from:

THE BARBERS, HAIRSTYLING FOR MEN, INC.

1316-730 Building, 730-2nd Avenue South Minneapolis, Minnesota, 55402 332-0469

The original stock offering advertisement from the St. Paul Pioneer Press, Sunday, March 30, 1969.

Joe receives “Upper Midwest Barber of the Year,” 1966.

Family vacation, 1967. L/R John, Joe, Jeanne, Barbara, Joey, Flo and Susan.

Looking for all the publicity they could get, Joe and Flo had an idea...reporters responded fast when Flo Francis asked if they'd care to cover a story about Joe and his five barbers giving simultaneous "first haircuts" to six one-year-olds. Radio announcers also showed up for the event.

Great publicity, six one-year-olds get first haircut.
From Minneapolis Tribune paper, 1968.

The Barbers new store in downtown Minneapolis, MN, 1970.

Francis family in the early years, 1974.

Joe, 1983 (shirt, compliments of Flo).

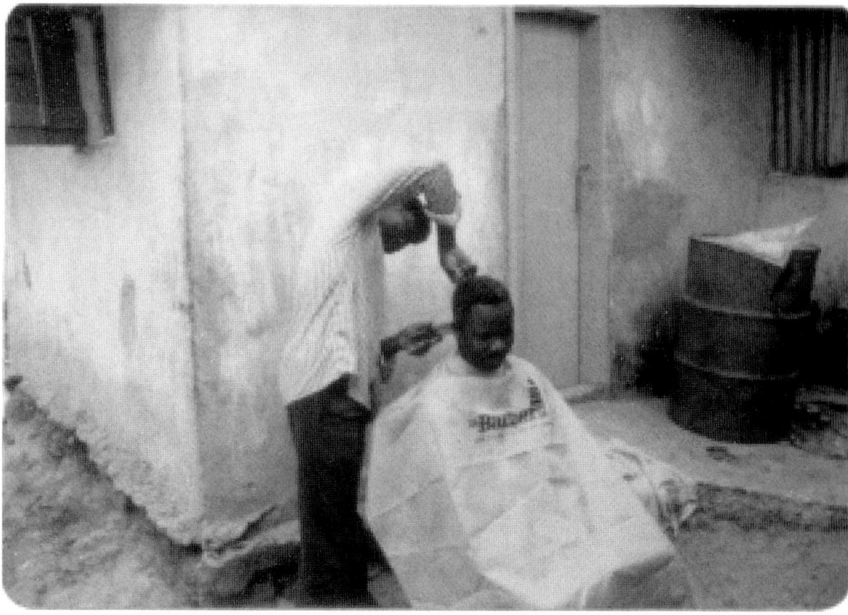

Joe visits a barber shop in Liberia, West Africa, 1976.

Flo, Joe and Miss France at City Looks
(St. Algue Salons) Conference in Paris, 1992.

10

BUSINESS

SUNDAY

The Barber of Moscow

With an eye on international franchising, Joe Francis of The Barbers is getting ready to open the first American beauty salon in the Soviet Union. Key to his plan: Soviet partners, a Soviet consultant and limited financial risk for himself.

Joe goes to Moscow.

John Francis—caught in a military coup in Moscow, Russia, 1992.

City Looks opens in Moscow, 1992.

Joe accepting the International Franchise Association
"Entrepreneur of the Year" award, 1992.

The Barber World Headquarters at 300 Industrial Boulevard,
Minneapolis, Minnesota.

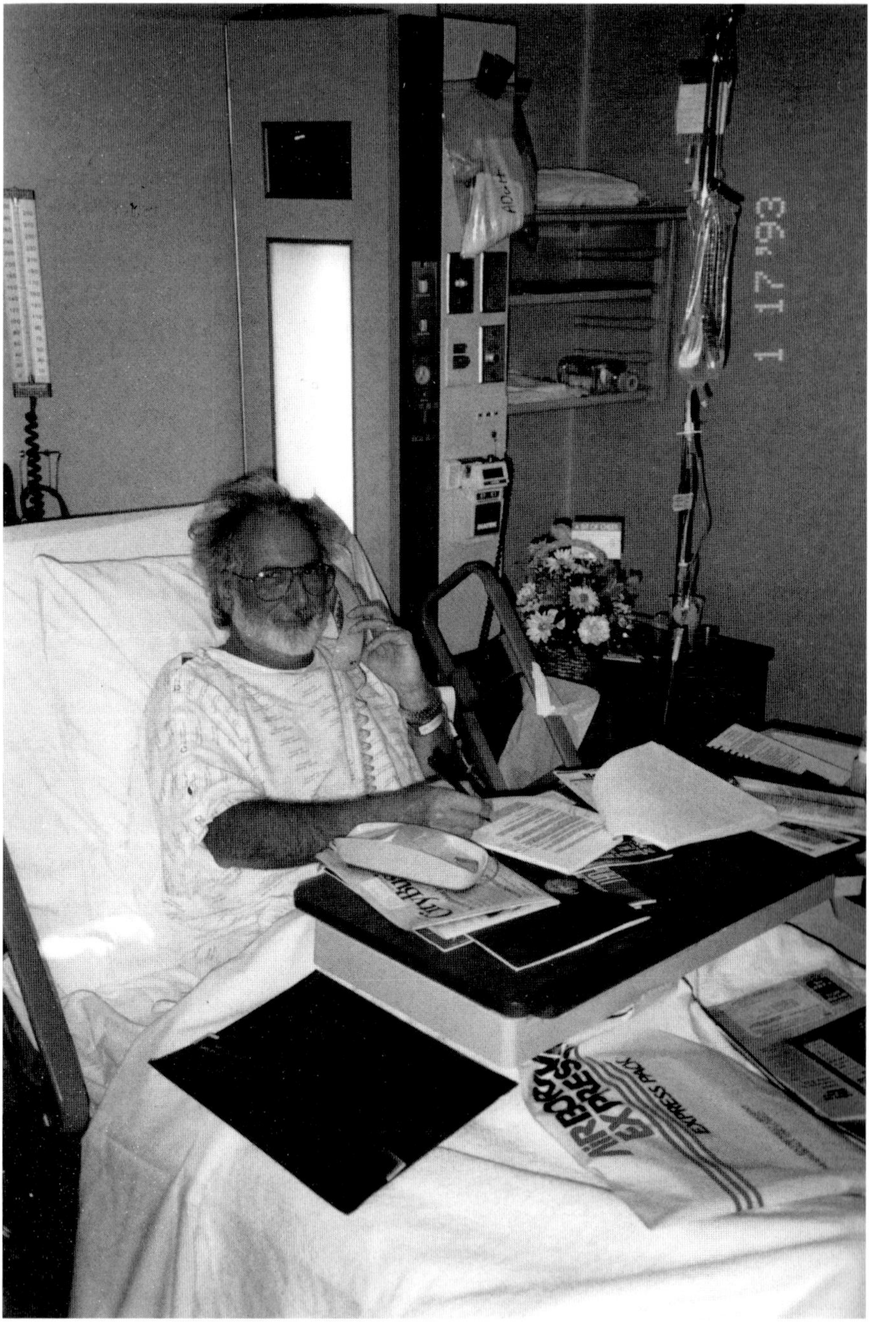

Joe often worked from his hospital bed, post surgery.
This was taken after his 20th surgery, 1993.

L/R Joey's son Joe Jr., Joey, Joe and Joe's mother Sadie, February 1994.

The playhouse Joe built for his grandkids.

Flo and John in Russia, 1996.

Flo and daughter Barb with Russian Salon partners.
L/R Zoya, Flo, Valentina and Barb, 1996.

THE Barbers®
Hairstyling for Men & Women Inc.

COST CUTTERS®
FAMILY HAIR CARE

City Looks Salons
International®

we care hair®

The four brands franchised by the Barbers Corporation.

Flo with her children. L/R Joey, Susan, Barb, Jeanne and John, 1996.

Flo with Board of Directors. L/R Flo, Jim Reissner, Richard King, Marcia Bystrom, Susan (Francis) Goldstein, David Emerson and Fred Huggins, 1997.

Joey Francis, firstborn in the Francis family,
died March 9, 1997.

Corporate Report features Flo as Chairman of the Board, 1997.

CHAPTER 9

A NEW DECADE

In 1990, with Joe at the helm, franchise owners and the Board are concerned that he is terminally ill, what to do? Joe was setting up a travel itinerary; he planed to visit franchisees and meet their staffs. Without consulting the Board about hiring, Joe once again went over their heads and appointed an Executive Vice President and two-person, in-house management committee to run the company while he was away. Not good! These three appointees created havoc, started making up their own rules and taking control. Joe realized his mistake and took corrective action. He could dismiss them as fast as he hired them. He took control again as the company continued to operate.

New CEO

There was an IFA meeting in Hawaii that Joe and Flo planned to attend. Fred Huggins had moved to Georgia and was setting up a consulting company. His position with the Mr. Donut franchise group was eliminated when the parent company sold that entire division. Fred was also attending the IFA meeting. His plan was to tell Joe he was going to be too busy to continue serving on The Barbers Board of Directors. Joe was wracked with pain from another surgery he'd endured just a few weeks before this. He didn't know about Fred's intentions and had asked Flo to find Fred and have him meet with them in their room. Flo had convinced Joe to approach Fred to stay on with the company and become their CEO.

When Fred arrived, Joe was resting on the bed. Joe and Flo asked if Fred would consider the CEO position. Fred knew there was no money to pay him for the job and he had witnessed too many situations where Joe refused to acquiesce his power. But Huggins also saw the magnitude of potential the company had. If it was managed properly and the growth was financially controlled, this could be a huge opportunity. He reminded Joe about the pay-out problems with the previous CEO and told Joe the company couldn't pay another salary. He proposed taking the position and receiving only stock in lieu of a salary for the next six months. Joe and Flo were surprised and pleased that Fred would consider this.

However, Fred needed complete financial and operational control of the company. He said they'd concentrate on a strategic plan together for The Barbers organization. He also said Joe couldn't hire staff or begin new projects without Huggins' approval. And that would only happen if it was part of their strategic plan. One of Joe's greatest fears was loss of control. On the other hand, he could face up to his situation and he knew Fred was qualified and familiar with the entire situation. Fred *was* the man for the job. Counseling with Flo, Joe agreed; Fred Huggins became CEO and president of The Barbers. Joe would remain Chairman of the Board.

Joe wrote in the 1990 Annual Report: "We saw immediate results when Fred Huggins joined our management team as President and CEO. He made a noticeable impact on our financial stats this fiscal year. Fred's lengthy experiences in national franchise management, knowledge of the industry and management style have made it easy for me to relinquish the position of President."

Huggins was a professional with extensive education and experience. He believed in strategic planning and follow through, and made people accountable for results. His background and contacts in the industry proved to be especially valuable as he brought talented leadership in with him.

While Huggins was at the helm, Joe earned national recognition that would also perpetuate the company's growth. In 1990 Joe was presented with the *Entrepre-*

neur of the Year award by Inc. Magazine. It was very prestigious. Ernst & Young, Merrill Lynch and Inc. Magazine sponsored this award. It might well have been the most important marketing event in the history of the company. This award lead to an international presence and increased credibility. The year came to an end with 500 salons in place, 414 of these were "Cost Cutters."

Pressing on with his strategic plans, Huggins said in 1991, "We are a franchised salon company and our focus will remain on building and servicing our franchises." He planned to reduce the number of corporate salons but to keep some as their laboratory for the continued development of the "City Looks" and "Cost Cutters" concepts. The focus was on being the finest franchised hair salon company in North America. They would accomplish this through preplanned direction, consistency and unparalleled service to their franchise network. An impressive number of services were put into place that year to enable franchisees to operate more profitably and manage their finances with improved, customized software and training.

Well, an old friend is back now—Wal-Mart. They revamped and rewrote their initial project, Hyper-Mart USA. It was now the *Super Center Store* concept and was expanding fast. A competitor, Fantastic Sam's, was going into some of the new locations. Fred Huggins sent in his vice president of Franchise Sales and Development, John Fox, a long-time business associate and co-worker from other franchise systems. Fox was a skilled negotiator and he was able to cut a deal with Wal-Mart.

They gave "Cost Cutters" the test sites of Savannah, Georgia and Chubbuck, Idaho to put salons in. These locations proved to be valuable additions to the Wal-Mart concept and a year later, there were nine more Cost Cutters salons in Wal-Mart Super Stores.

Things were much improved from the original salons of a couple of years back. In the third year with Wal-Mart, "Cost Cutters" opened in over 100 locations. In fact, there was a day, *one single day* that saw 25 new "Cost Cutters" salons opened, a feat unheard of in The Barbers history. Ultimately, there would be 350 "Cost Cutters" salons in Wal-Mart Super Stores. Several franchisees from Joe's *old guard,* including Bill Kaminski, Jim Curran, Dave Flat and Randy Butts, developed large areas with many multiple units over the years, within Wal-Mart locations. The Wal-Mart deal was an absolutely remarkable achievement that added credibility, momentum and cash as well. It pushed The Barbers ahead at lightening speed. Flo credits John Fox's ability to deal effectively with Wal-Mart as one of The Barbers most important achievements.

Joe was gravely ill at this point but still working everyday. And unless you asked the man about his health, it was never a topic. He always maintained an interest in his business and in other people. Anyone you could talk to, that was well-acquainted with Joe, would tell you the same thing—he was always about everyone else, not about himself.

CHAPTER 10

MOSCOW

In 1989, Joe read an article in the Wall Street Journal that solicited business leaders to apply for a trip to Moscow on a first ever U.S. business trade mission. With the ending of the cold war in the late 1980s, Joe was endlessly curious and optimistic about the opening of markets in Eastern Europe. Applicants would be considered to represent U.S. businesses after paying a $15,000 fee. He was intrigued, applied and was accepted. The trade mission was a very controlled process, as the Soviet, Communist wall was not yet down. Sponsors of this mission included, amongst others: the United States-State Dept., US Chamber of Commerce, General Motors, Cargill and other fortune 500 companies. No doubt, Joe's considerable business recognition, achievements and awards impressed the selection committee.

When he returned from this trade mission, Joe was impressed with the range of opportunities and had already visualized his company doing business in Russia. He shared his enthusiasm with his youngest son, John, who was a recent college graduate. Joe said "we're going to Russia, here's an opportunity for you if you want it. I need you to do some research and learn all you can about how we can do business in Russia." John went to his alma mater—the University of St. Thomas in St. Paul, MN and discovered that the International Business Development department could direct him to more resources. John knew, just like Flo, that when he saw the twinkle in his dad's eye regarding this matter, he may as well be proactive, and help.

The recently opened World Trade Center, located in downtown St. Paul, had an impressive International Resource Department. John was able to meet and begin networking with many business people who had experience in dealing with Russia and other foreign countries. Armed with everything he could glean from these sources and contacts, John worked with Joe to find business prospects abroad. Months into the project and lacking any traction to get something moving, Joe came across another local entrepreneur, who had started a pen-pal program for the countries of Hungary, Poland and Czechoslovakia. Joe found this man to be a person-to-person, focused matchmaker and offered to buy his business related contact letters for the next year.

John Francis: "It was unbelievable, Dad offered him $500 for all his business related letters for a full year. He sent me over there to pick them up. There were literally boxes and boxes of letters. I put them in my car, went back over to dad's house and we started going through them, looking for any and all that were in English." Joe really didn't know what he was going to do with these. There was no plan, just endless curiosity and optimism. They decided to start a letter mailing response. John made up a form letter to respond to those that they both felt had any potential. A salon business-contacts-prospecting-plan was in motion for the eastern European markets.

At that time, these countries had just started to open up. International business interest was exploding. Gorbachev had come to Minnesota for an official and public visit, there was local and international publicity regarding the Eastern block opening up and you couldn't hold Joe down. He knew he was on to something! His enthusiasm was contagious and Norm Stoehr, Joe's business partner with "Inner Circle," introduced Joe to Mark Grin, a recent Russian immigrant who was new to Minnesota. Mark was trying to make better use of his contacts in Moscow. Joe liked Grin and offered him an office and all the support he needed, to focus on getting The Barbers some Russian business partners in the salon business there. In return, Joe would help Grin find U.S. prospects for other business contacts.

Mark Grin was a state-trained Economist in Russia. He hated the Communist model and had come to America just a few years earlier. He had no idea how friendly and intimate the office atmosphere Joe was setting him up with would be. He would share space in a small office with John, at the Barbers headquarters. Needless to say, this was a surprise to John too. Working nearly face to face was not easy for them, Mark could be very loud and could ignite during a phone call, when talking to his Russian connections. John, a more easy-going, laid-back and controlled man, was sometimes challenged in this environment. Their work continued and John pursued every lead while Mark worked his contacts.

Meantime, Joe Francis got a tremendous boost in credibility due to his considerable business acumen. This was when Joe received the *Entrepreneur of the Year* award from *Inc. Magazine.* This was huge and resulted in some incredible and immediate publicity. Mark had lined up eight prospective salon business partners in Russia and Joe told him to set up a trip to Moscow. Before they left, Mark contacted all the Moscow media he could find to tell them he was bringing the "American Entrepreneur of the Year" to Moscow, in search of business partners. Moscow was hungry for aggressive, capital-producing ideas and intrigued with entrepreneurship.

Not everyone was crazy about Joe's propensity to enter the global market. Some of the Board meetings regarding this matter were pretty lively at times. The Board struggled to keep up with Joe. They were asking; what about our domestic system's needs, problems and issues—why Russia? Perhaps Joe subscribed to this quote from Henri Amiel: *"Analysis kills spontaneity...the grain once ground into flour, germinates no more."* Joe knew what was going on, he understood his limitations and that's why he had all these people around him. Let *them* manage. Let *them* organize; he was about the horizon and what's beyond. The day-to-day operation was in good hands and didn't provide Joe with the same stimulation and enthusiasm as the opening of huge, new world markets. The endless opportunities that were so obvious to Joe were like a drug for him, they gave him drive and vision.

When Joe and Mark first arrived in Russia in late 1990, they stayed at Mark's mother's apartment. She moved in with her other son to give them room to work. During the next nine days, Mark had Joe booked with radio, TV and newspapers. They all wanted to interview the "American Entrepreneur of the Year." This was all free, priceless publicity, earned through Joe's recognition and awards.

The TV audience numbered 90 million viewers in several different countries. Joe was very relaxed and the audiences loved this handsome, dapper and successful man from America who was looking for Russian business partners. These were prime-time TV shows and Joe came across like a Hollywood star.

The most popular Moscow newspapers; Pravda and Isvestia carried Joe's stories. An emerging business paper, Kommersant, came to interview Joe in St. Petersburg. The publicity was monumental and Joe told the viewers that he wanted to find some Russian partners within the next 90 days and get a Salon up and running within six months. Joe and Mark met with the eight prospective partners Mark had lined up and then Joe headed back to the States. Mark was to stay a few more days to tie up loose ends and then return also, but some salon business owners, who caught part of Joe's interviews on TV, called the American Embassy in Moscow for contact information for Joe and The Barbers.

They called Minneapolis and Joe put them in contact with Mark, who was still in Moscow. As a result, another trip to Moscow was arranged and if successful, a trip for the Russians to come for a meeting in Minneapolis would be planned. The Barbers offered to cover expenses. Within a few months, the Russians met at The Barbers headquarters. The Russian contingent was composed of two women, Valentina Valentukevich and Zoya Schkott, who directed health and personal grooming in Russia and their male partner, Vladimir Klubkov. They had the industry experience, reputation, customer contacts and a perfect location for a salon. John had found a special local attorney with experience in Russian law to draft the joint-venture agreement. The Barbers were to provide expertise, products, equipment and management training; the Russians would provide the location, working capital and management to operate the business. Profits would be split on a 50/50 basis. At that time, Russian citizens couldn't own real estate, but this Moscow team had a ninety-nine year lease on a building that might work for a salon. It was about a half-mile east of the Kremlin, in downtown Moscow, not far from Red Square.

The negotiating looked like a stand off. The Russians would not sign the deal at The Barbers headquarters. Typical to Russian style and unusual for Americans, they took their time. They dragged it out until Joe had driven them out to the Minneapolis/St. Paul International airport for their return to Moscow. They finally signed the deal in the car before their departure. Next step, Joe told Mark and John; "Go over there and get us set up—do whatever it takes." This is quite an exciting opportunity for John, a 23-year-old man just a couple years out of college. So John, always willing to face a challenge and anxious to show his dad he could get it done, made plans to head for Moscow. Joe had tremendous confidence in John. After all, John had a great track record. Starting as one of six one year olds getting their hair cut for a publicity stunt in 1967, John was "on call" through his Jr. High, Sr. High and College years. He'd experienced everything from putting flyers out to cleaning, painting, grass cutting, delivering product to salons, being involved in the family video games business, managing Joe's real estate properties, and working his way up through various company departments. Some people called him "The Clean-up Kid."

In August, 1991 John arrived in Moscow to begin the planning process. He'd have to negotiate with the Russians; Valentina, in her 50s, Zoya, in her 40s and Vladimir in his 30s, as to which products and equipment would go into this salon and what was needed to open.

Pricing for the haircut and styling was another serious consideration. When Joe priced the razor cut, in the early 1960s, at over three times what regular haircuts were going for—the local barbers didn't think he could pull it off. But in Moscow, the set-up team figured they'd be able to charge about $100 dollars per treatment or service. The salon was targeting the top levels of Moscovites, not average working people.

While John was in the hotel meeting room going through catalogs, pictures of equipment and helping the new partners make plans, a military coup was initiated. Gorbachev got thrown out of power and Boris Yeltsin came in. There was chaos and havoc, military vehicles, tanks and soldiers all over the streets of Moscow. The American embassy suggested that all Americans get out of Moscow immediately.

John had an interpreter and driver named Victor, a friend of Mark Grin. Victor assured John there's nothing to worry about; he'll take good care of him. He recommends they leave the hotel and John should come to stay with him at his home. No problem, John's OK with all of this, so they take off for Victor's home. Now, Victor lives north of the city quite a ways out. Since it will be a long drive and everyone is hungry, they decide to see if they can find a restaurant that is still serving. Not far from the hotel, they find a restaurant and are seated near the front window. Vodka is brought to the table, glasses are raised—Cheers! They observe people running in the streets, setting up improvised barricades across the streets and things were starting to look very ominous.

After dinner, Victor's posture has changed, he thinks it's time to get out of town. As they motor along side streets, looking for an outlet, they're stopped by a group of soldiers. Victor tells John to give him his passport. Victor flashes John's USA passport in the face of the commanding soldier, screams at him in Russian and they are waved through. Victor had told the soldier that John was an American diplomat and that Victor and his party were assigned to get him out of town.

Meantime, back in the states, Flo is totally beside herself with fear for her son. She has not been able to get through by telephone since all lines are busy or torn down. Her son is in the middle of what would be a three-day coup in Russia. Flo continues calling and after nearly 24 hours finally locates John, insisting that he get out of there and come home. John tells Flo that all is well, he's at Victor's and everything is fine, no problems. It will all die down in a day or two—he's not coming home, he has work to do.

The coup past, John completed his initial consulting and the build-out process began. The salon was not finished until June of 1992 and went way over budget. It was gorgeous with crystal chandeliers, marble floors, granite counters, a full bar, new stylists, facialists, masseurs, and various spa specialists, ready to open. John hired one of The Barbers franchisees, Scott Russell, from Green Bay, Wisconsin to go over with him to help train the staff stylists. John helped with the Customer Service training and product sales. They spent three weeks helping their Russian partners get up and running in July, 1992. The Grand Opening was spectacular. However, about 3-4 months after opening, when John came back to check on them, things seemed to sour—the honeymoon was over. Valentina informed John that their agreement is unenforceable and they got what they wanted and no longer need him or The Barbers. They really got right in John's face and basically told him there was nothing he could do but leave. John protested their underhandedness.

John was astonished and incredulous. He came back and sat down with Joe, telling him he felt like a failure. But this is Joe Francis he's talking with. Joe tells him, "You did a good job, John, you got the thing open and we weren't sure that was ever going to happen. You got it done—don't worry, we'll work this out." Mark Grin got on the phone and soon went over for a visit.

The Russians were resistant. They told Grin they would only deal with Joe. They didn't want the young kid; they wanted the gray-haired father. So Joe went over and started to negotiate. Then he told John he wanted him to go back with him on the next trip. John had been there sixteen times but this would be the only time he was there with his dad. Joe was gravely ill by this time but wouldn't relent to the disease and they made the trip together. The relationship with these Russians was still waning.

When they arrived in Moscow, the Russians had arranged for them to stay in an old monastery that had been renovated. Donislevsky Monastery was now a beautiful hotel. Apparently, the stage was being set for reconciliation, due to the threats of legal action and equipment removal John had proposed during the previous trip. The Moscow salon was very successful and John was anxious to get the business deal back on track. Joe told them about his illness, and that if it was the last thing he did, he wanted to make the deal work. This made a very positive impact on the Russian partners, they had mutual respect for each other.

While they were there, John observed the clientele coming into the salon. He realized these people were wealthy—famous singers, actors, military and government leaders, business leaders...these were people of means and influence. The salon prices were sky-high but the clients were glad to pay. This City Looks Salon was top shelf, as good as it gets, nothing like it in Moscow at the time.

Later, John would say the relationship would not have been put back on track without Joe's intervention. It all worked out, apologies made, hugs all around and some cash paid by the Moscow salon. Should be "OK" now? Not quite. Although they did collect some overdue cash, the Russians would continue to renege on their obligations after Joe's meeting with them.

Then, a strategic change of events occurred. Much of the industry in the former Soviet Union was being privatized. The government dismantled the old structure and informed the Salon owners they were now independently-owned collectives. They now own their salons—they no longer belong to the government. It was the beginning of free enterprise and John saw past the horizon, he had a winning card in his hand. Now, he had a strategy that could resolve this knotty problem with the City Looks partners.

What John saw was the opportunity to distribute The Barbers products, other salon equipment and supplies to all other independent salons. This would mean that the Moscow City Looks Salon was not exclusive—*unless* they cooperated. The Barbers had exclusive rights to some world famous product brands; most notably, the Paul Mitchell products. The Barbers 30 year relationship with Paul Mitchell had earned them exclusivity.

Further, John had become familiar with and friends with many of the Russians, including some in the media. What if he exposed the Russian City Looks partner's dishonesty? What if he exposed the Russian City Looks salon partners for what they were? He knew that bad publicity like this would destroy their reputations, business and possibly their futures in the industry. They started to listen.

When they initially set up the Moscow salon, they negotiated with chair and equipment manufacturers and product suppliers to help fund the set-up. The salon's chairs were owned by the manufacturers; they were the lien holders. Much of the decor and products were also provided by other lien holders. Consequently, John hired a guy to come into the salon and give him an estimate for removing the chairs and equipment. He told the Russians, "If you refuse to work with us, then I'm going to have to take this salon apart and I want all our equipment back." He walked around the salon pointing at various things saying: "This goes, that goes, take these mirrors, and yank out these work stations" etc. Valentina came over to see what was going on. He introduced her to this guy and then told her "I'm just explaining how wonderful our business partnership is and I'm pointing out to him what we contributed." (A ploy familiar to the Russians.) She knew what was going on but really didn't know if this was a bluff or the real thing.

John hadn't made the decision yet to go through with the stripping of the Salon and returned to the States. Then, a strange thing happened. About a week later, the guy John hired for the moving estimate called the salon. He's at the Moscow Salon to remove the equipment. He's got questions, somehow, there was a misunderstanding. Valentina then realized that John had been serious and this would be the worst outcome for her salon.

The Russians suggested that John come back and they patch up everything. This time they said "We never intended for you to go away." John wasn't going to fall for any more false promises. He'd learned that Russian laws had changed and foreign firms could now own their businesses in Russia; he could set up other salons if they didn't cooperate. He went back over and cut a new deal. They'd pay The Barbers $10,000 per month and he'd have to get six months in advance. They wrote a wire transfer for $60,000, signed a new agreement and would continue to honor it from that point. Joe was in the hospital when John came back with the money. Some of the people at The Barbers had been calling the Moscow deal "Joe's Folly." Joe was really happy that John put this deal to rest!

John had learned many valuable "relationship" lessons while working with his Dad. Even though he'd come back home with a stack of cash, he wanted the Russians to be happy and he wanted to avoid anything like the previous scenario. A few months later, more beauty product distribution in Russia was considered by The Barbers and their Russian partners. As a result of a conversation between Fred Huggins and Luke Jacobellis, the president of the Paul Mitchell Company, John learned that Luke wanted to meet with the Moscow salon owners regarding product distribution in Russia. He wanted them to come into the company headquarters in California so that he could explain to them what the Paul Mitchell systems business was all about. They all flew into Los Angeles, met with John and Fred Huggins and went over to Paul Mitchell headquarters. The group spent a day and a half at the facility and the company threw a reception for the Russians. After this, John arranged for them to spend a weekend in Las Vegas.

It was an important part of rebuilding their relationship. John sincerely wanted to make amends. It was a wake-up call for the Russians. He told them they just had to see Las Vegas. Since travel by train was the way to go in Russia, John arranged an afternoon ride on

Amtrak from LA to Las Vegas. They had a great time telling stories. John's Russian was getting a little better and their English was improving as well. With a little vodka as refreshment, it was a fun ride!

Once in Las Vegas, they wanted to experience a Water Park and John accommodated. They saw "Splash" at the Riviera and everyone thoroughly enjoyed the entertainment. As a result of this interaction, the relationship became much warmer and stabilized. Their difficulties had passed and mutual respect was restored. The Russian business was maintained and grew to expand to other salons and training facilities in Russia, with distribution of products and supplies.

"Just go get it done, John. Do whatever it takes."

Joe Francis

CHAPTER 11

GLOBAL GROWTH

During an IFA Trade Mission in 1991, while the build-out for the Moscow salon was in motion, Joe, Flo and John traveled to London where a Franchise show would give them exposure to the market in England. Unfortunately for The Barbers, there was a huge shake-up and scandal in the hair industry in England. Just prior to the Trade Mission, some London-based hair salon franchise company had failed its franchisees. There were rumors of graft and corruption within that organization and investors avoided the salon industry which was well out of favor at that time in the UK.

But the trade mission included another stop, this time in Paris. This would prove to be an enormous stroke of luck for The Barbers. While at the Paris meeting, executives representing Saint Algue, a hair salon franchise chain operating in France, visited The Barbers booth. What was remarkable was that Saint Algue really mirrored the structure at The Barbers. It was run by the founder, Gerard Glemain, who was a successful hairdresser close to Joe's age.

This company had upscale salons but was trying to develop another brand, similar to Cost Cutters. They had not been successful and were searching for a solution. John checked on them through the IFA and the US Embassy, and a meeting was set up for the next day. They found the similarities in philosophy, structure and customer service to be amazing. The thing that was missing was the Cost Cutter business format and product sales. The Saint Algue company needed help establishing a second brand, and a business plan for the secondary market.

A meeting was set up for a visit to the United States by the St. Algue top echelon. They met with Joe, CEO Fred Huggins and other staff members of The Barbers and toured several salons. This was more a fact-finding mission for St. Algue than a trip to consummate a working arrangement. About a month later, Joe and Fred made a trip to close the deal at St. Algue's headquarters in Paris. They traveled by train to the company's most successful salon in Rennes, France. Both were impressed with what they saw. Back in Paris, the two companies came to an agreement and Master Franchise contracts were signed, to develop a chain of Cost Cutter-style salons, using the brand name of "City Looks." Their goal was to expand from their present 200 Saint Algue salons in France and Switzerland, by adding another 100 "City Looks" salons within five years.

In 1992, their first City Looks Salon Grand Opening was in Torcy, France, a Paris suburb. This was a very successful start and quickly created an impetus for many more City Looks salon openings that followed. Recognizing an ambitious and aggressive corporate culture within St. Algue, The Barbers granted St. Algue a Master Franchise agreement that would allow them to expand to several other E.U. countries. The deal gave The Barbers overnight expansion potential of unusual proportion and, along with Moscow, made them a sophisticated international franchise player. Joe knew this move would result in a large dose of fabulous publicity. It did.

This franchise relationship made a huge contribution to The Barbers credibility and growth. The shops in France were expanding at the same time the Moscow Salon was taking off. The press for these events was tremendous and pushed The Barbers to new and exciting heights in the early to mid 1990s. The Barbers also acquired another domestic chain of salons in the Chicago area. An upscale, full-service salon group, Hair Performers, had 61 salons and sold to The Barbers in April of 1992. The company converted 23 of these locations to their City Looks concept.

During a later trip to visit the French franchise organization, Joe and Fred were guests of Gerard Glemain, at his condominium in the French Alps at Mount Blanc. They were treated like royalty.

They finished their visit and were planning to return to the States, when Joe became extremely ill. Fred noticed that Joe's color had faded and he could barely stand, so they were off to the local hospital. The doctors there contacted Mayo Clinic in Minnesota and Fred got Joe on a plane for an immediate flight back. During the flight, Joe had a severe internal bleeding episode and was laid out on the floor of the DC-10. There was a doctor on board from Norway who was also headed for the Mayo Clinic and he helped to stabilize Joe. Once back in Minneapolis, Flo rushed him by ambulance to the clinic in Rochester. Another close call.

Joe, though gravely ill at this point, was still working everyday. And unless you asked the man about his health, it was never a topic. He always maintained an interest in his business and in other people.

In 1993, the "Super Cuts" salon chain approached Joe to buy his company. Joe figured the company was worth about $11 or $12 million dollars. He hired accounting consultants who came up with a $6 million figure. The tab for this evaluation was $100,000. Fred Huggins was not happy with this unplanned cost. He felt they had enough in-house talent to do this without paying a fee, but it was too late, Joe had already gone ahead with it. Joe, had been used to total autonomy all through the years. His concern for his family could easily overshadow his better judgment. The timeline for his health too—how much time did he have? He just didn't know.

After "Super Cuts" looked over the evaluation, they offered the company only $3 million. This was not realistic and really knocked the wind out of Joe's sails! There was no way he'd sell at that price. He didn't know at that time whether he had days, weeks or months left to live. Joe told his daughter, Susan Goldstein, that he wanted to get the company sold so that Flo wouldn't have to deal with it. When Jim Reissner, former banker, joined The Barbers board, Joe had told him "my days are numbered and I need someone I can trust to support Flo through this." (Super Cuts would be back later with a better offer.)

The company was getting huge by now, with the system-side sales at $123 million for 1993. But net income was no where near what they needed. Joe thought some fresh publicity might help the cause. One morning, he called the local papers and started a rumor that the company was contemplating another stock split. The next day, it was all over the papers. Fred Huggins was alarmed, and he told Joe, "You can't do that, we're a public company and there are rules, ethics, boundaries—you can't do this kind of thing Joe!"

Joe replied, "I thought it might be a good idea—to demonstrate our value."

While sympathetic to Joe's suffering and anxiety, Fred, for the benefit of the business, really tightened the clamps on Joe. Joe was thinking he had only months left to get Flo out with cash and dignity—maybe he had only weeks left? Regardless of his medical condition,

Joe was still looking to grow the company and was aware of everything that was going on.

In June of 1993, the company purchased 22 Family Haircut Stores in New England and converted most of these to the Cost Cutters' concept. Joe wrote in the annual report that year that this acquisition would create a strong presence for expanding growth opportunities in the New England market. The Barbers closed the year with more fabulous publicity. *Success* magazine recognized the top franchise companies—the "Gold 100" in the United States. The Barbers ranked #15 among the top 100 of more than 4,000 franchise companies in North America.

The company also celebrated their 30th Anniversary in 1993. The gala event was attended by corporate staff and franchisees from across the country, as well as the French partners.

JoAnne Shaw, a friend and business associate, and her husband Julius, owned the national franchise system, "The Coffee Beanery," based in Michigan. They met Joe Francis in the late 1980s at an International Franchise Association (IFA) convention. Joe felt that the IFA board of directors needed a woman with JoAnne's background and Joe talked with her about it. Subsequent to that meeting, Joe nominated JoAnne, to be a member of the IFA Board. Within a couple of years, she was invited to become a Board member and she accepted. She went on to become the first woman to be Chairman of The Board of the IFA. She was invited to speak at The Barbers Silver Anniversary event. Joanne said it was inspiring to see how Joe's franchisees loved him. She also mentioned that Joe always spoke about his franchisees with admiration and respect.

By 1994, things were looking pretty good, except for Joe's health. He had surgeries every three to four months in 1990-1994, and began weekly blood transfusions in 1994. He suffered greatly but he tried to keep his chin up and not let it show.

One of Joe's close associates, Rick Goldberg, had been thinking about Joe's generosity in helping others. Rick knew that Joe didn't have much time left and he had an idea to run by him. The two had met years before when Rick came in for an interview to go to work with The Barbers in the 1980s. Rick had been in the Bond field and didn't know if the Salon business would be sophisticated enough to hold his interest. When he met Joe, he found him to be a very warm, stately man with an abundance of energy. After meeting with Joe and learning more about the company's success and plans for the future, he knew he was in the right place.

Rick's tenure with the company and getting to know Joe much better on a personal basis, led him to make a phone call to set up a meeting with him in 1994. Rick: "Joe, you gave me a shot when no one else would. In my mind and in the mind of hundreds of others, you're a legend. Your vision, your wisdom and contributions, I mean—these are really important things. What if we started a fund, Joe? I remember how you had to shine shoes to get money to go to Barber school. Wouldn't it be neat if some deserving people out there could apply to a foundation that would help them pay for going to a Barber or Beauty school?"

Joe's heart was aflame again. He loved the idea. They set up an organizational and management board just before Joe died. Later, after his death, with Flo as chairman, and their daughter Susan as president, the start-up fund raising began. Susan, spearheaded the task and worked The Barbers conventions and trade shows to establish the fund. She was successful in short order, raising over $250,000 through her efforts. Most of Joe's franchisees were happy to donate. Several of them gave tens of thousands of dollars in memory of Joe. Today, the 'Joe Francis Scholarship Foundation' lives on, chaired by Flo. Each year, hundreds of applicants are evaluated. From 1997 to 2007, 116 students received $1,000 each. In 2008, 18 $1,000 grants were awarded. Flo's daughter, Barb, joined the Foundation as the new President in 2002. Just as this endeavor was precious to Joe, it remains the same with Flo and the family. They love to see recipients benefit from Joe's spirit living on.

Rick Goldberg: "This was something that gave the many people, who had prospered through their affiliation with Joe, a means of giving back spiritually. It's something they could do that was meaningful for Joe and Flo and the rest of the family. It really touched Joe. He was the classic entrepreneur, always passionate in what he did. Flo was his rock—always! They came up from the streets the hard way. They appreciated everything they had and never took it for granted. While Joe was out slaying dragons, Flo was tending the home fires.

But at the end of the day, they always met around the campfire and really took care of each other. Their relationship was remarkable."

CHAPTER 12

WATERING THE TREE

"Go for it!"—My husband's last words to the surgeon, April 14, 1994.

Florence Francis

It was a nice spring day...birds chirping, sun shining, mid-afternoon and Joe and Flo are in the family backyard. Flo noticed Joe watering a small tree. The tree has been dead for months. She asked Joe, "What on earth are you doing watering this tree? It's dead." Joe said "it'll come back." Flo reached over, grabbed the frail little trunk and gently lifted it right out of the ground. Even the roots had dried up. "It can't come back Joe, it's completely dead."

Joe Francis was about three years from his own death at that time. But just as he always expected his darkest days to come into light, and just as he expected that people around him who struggled would come back strong; he did expect that tree could come back too.

Nothing in his challenging upbringing would offer any evidence that this man would become a staunch optimist. There were many adverse events throughout his life that would have turned most optimists into pessimists. But, for whatever reason, Joe maintained his titanium core...he had educated his heart to believe things will always get better.

He'd been told by doctors he would be gone by now. According to them, he was supposed to be dead two years ago. His peaks and valleys in the struggle with cancer took place over a period of twelve years and 23 surgeries. One year, Joe endured five operations and still went to work after each of them. Everyone who witnessed the battle just couldn't believe how Joe fought back. Moreover, how he could leave the operating table and return to work within days. (You have to wonder what Joe thought when an employee would call in sick... "Can't make it in today—too sick?")

His struggle with health likely had its start in Africa. Joe and Flo loved to travel and wanted their children to have a greater perspective on what the world was all about. Through trips abroad, they witnessed everything from abject poverty to wealth and royalty. In 1976, they all traveled to Liberia, Africa to visit Flo's brother, Bud. He had become a missionary after he left the Marquardt family bakery. The visit in Africa included many excursions into the jungle, where the family of seven stayed in native huts. Quite an experience for everyone, rats running up the walls and across the ceiling, dirt floor for sleeping, insects, bad food, one bucket of water daily for bathing and the feeling of poverty all around. Flo said, "the realization that people living with literally nothing, were very happy, friendly and generous, was an invaluable and important lesson for us."

Apparently, Joe got tangled up with the wrong mosquito and two years later, in 1978, he became so ill he could barely function. Flo got him into the hospital for diagnostic tests and unfortunately, the diagnosis was incorrect. They determined he needed an exploratory operation. In the process his spleen was removed. But that didn't seem to help and doctors feared Joe was in the last stage of multiple tumors of his lymph nodes. Flo took him to the Mayo Clinic in an ambulance where they examined him and discovered he had Malaria. He was treated for this and soon felt much better. But five years later in 1982, troubled with gut-wrenching pain, Joe checked into the Mayo Clinic in Rochester and received life-threatening news. He was diagnosed as having a cancer tumor in one of his kidneys. It had to be operated on immediately. Post-operation, the doctors felt that they had gotten it all and told Joe the operation was a success.

Joe's daughter Susan: "I remember having Thanksgiving dinner at the Mayo Clinic, in dad's hospital room. He was so young, only 48 at the time."

Flo realized she'd have to remain strong in front of Joe and the kids. She would commute to and from Mayo Clinic, in Rochester, Minnesota, daily, often getting home from the hospital at two or three o'clock in the morning, exhausted and then, having repressed her feelings, fall totally apart.

Flo: "I was nearly out of my mind. I knew it was rare that the cancer *wouldn't* return. I discussed it with the doctors but didn't want to talk with Joe about it...him being such an optimist. So, as Joe thought, "I'm free of cancer," I agreed, but I knew chances were slim that it wouldn't come back—and of course, it did. I always wrote to the doctors to see what the next step would be if there was a reoccurrence, but I never shared this with Joe."

John Francis: "The first thing I remember about dad's sickness was when I was in the sixth grade. That's when they took out his spleen but then found out what he really had was Malaria. Years later, we were cutting down trees in our backyard...me, my dad, uncle and a couple other guys. We were cleaning up the mess and all of a sudden my dad got this sharp pain in his side. He went in and when he urinated, he said there was blood in it. We knew this was really serious. At the hospital, they discovered a cancerous tumor in one of his kidneys. That's when the whole cancer thing started."

Flo: "He was so courageous! I mean, he'd come out of an operation, be in the hospital for four or five days and go right back to work. Or he'd go to the airport for his next trip. He couldn't even drive; he'd be too weak!

So I'd drive him to the office, or John or Joey would take him in. We were all worried about him going back to work so soon but to no avail...that was Joe. Even people in the office would be upset to see Joe so weak...they knew he shouldn't be there and they knew he was in serious pain."

(Author's note:) What about physical pain—what do we know about pain? Can a simple headache, cold or the flu create a major change in behavior? Can you remember the last time you were at work and experienced some sort of exaggerated pain? For most of us, it changes everything. Pretty tough to have a cheery disposition and high interest in the job at hand when we can't get rid of the pain. Our interest in the welfare of others is likely to fade as well. But many of those who worked with and came into contact with Joe Francis would never know he was suffering abject pain...the man looked past his pain and into the future. And how is this possible? Apparently Joe knew what behaviorists have known for a long time...we're most unhappy when thinking of ourselves and most happy when we're thinking of others. Joe was always thinking about others and this author believes Joe was in a hurry to get his company into a very healthy state, even though he knew his own health was going in the wrong direction. I believe, from all the evidence available, that Joe was totally committed to and determined to leave a legacy of wealth for his sweetheart wife and beloved children. He knew he could pull it off before this dastardly disease would consume him.

What's more, Joe's passion to make a poor man rich provided him with plenty of other opportunity. So many of his dedicated staff and franchisees were on his mind. He wanted to put them in a position to greatly profit from years of turmoil, exhausting schedules and endless loyalty. Joe had to see them win too. If he was going down, all around him would rise. When you consider kidney and intestinal surgery, even if you've never suffered the experience, you just have to imagine how life-sapping it would be. You can't stand, sit, twist, cough, sneeze, lie down or get up without using your stomach muscles. Imagine getting cut open 23 times over twelve years. More than that, imagine being able to function like a champion while going through the process. No question about it...Joe Francis was not thinking about himself!

Jim Reissner, one of Joe's long-time bankers: "Joe called to set up a luncheon date. It was late into his illness and I noticed he wasn't eating much. I said, "Joe, you don't seem very hungry—you feeling OK?" Joe told me his cancer was getting worse—that he'd had some treatment and the prognosis wasn't good. He wanted me to join his Board of Directors, as he wanted some people around to look after things and support Flo. His plan was to have her succeed him in running the company. He was in extreme pain yet maintained his focus and clear thinking. He was thinking of his family and all the franchisees and staff. He said he knew that Flo was the best person to manage the business and wanted to surround her with people he knew he could trust.

Joe was always positive and he knew Flo would be a positive leadership choice for all his franchisees. He was a good strategic thinker and more concerned about other people than himself. He also knew his days were limited and that he was going to live with extreme pain for the rest of his life. He still maintained a positive attitude in spite of this and continued to work on strengthening the company while preparing for his demise. One of the brilliant decisions he made was to choose Flo as his successor. She had become vice-chair of the board for The Barbers in 1988 and after Joe's passing, was Chairman of the board.

Cheryl Babcock: "After Joe was gone, what I heard from my contacts in the Twin Cities area and through the IFA, is what a great guy Joe was but also what a savvy woman Flo was. Along with Joe, they had put a good team together and Flo was utilizing that team, made them dig deeper and did what *she* had to…to lead.

While Joe was still here, I loved seeing them together, at the IFA conventions or social and company events. You could see the pride they took in each other and that spark in their eyes. And to see them on the dance floor, just enjoying each other's company, it was like suddenly there wasn't anyone else there. They had so much pride in one another. Flo was dealing with a huge personal loss, but she also realized that the system was as well. So she had to be strong for her family, strong for herself and strong for the company. Flo was the glue that held everything together, not just her family but the franchise family as well."

Those working with Joe, the last few years of his life, felt he was always thinking about the company and his family. Many times you wouldn't know he was sick. His positive attitude, his endless energy...he was always well groomed and neatly dressed and probably exhausted at times. Joe was a true champion."

Joe knew he had to raise the bar for himself and get this company to the top before the clock ran out. God bless his golden heart...he would get the job done.

Joe's daughter, Jeanne: "Long into his illness, I was studying at the Art Institute of Chicago and dad had to go in for yet another operation. I wanted to take time off and come up to be with him but he said *"Hell no...Your life isn't going to stop just because I'm sick."* Dad was always my #1 cheerleader.

Well, I had been seeing a therapist in an effort to deal with my feelings about my dad's impending death. So, I asked dad if he could come down and meet with me and my therapist after the next operation. He said *"Sure."* So what does he do? He calls to say he'll be down right after the operation. That's exactly what he did. I picked him up at O'Hare International and he had to walk about a mile from the gate to where I was parked. His operation had been just a few days before and when he got into my car, he was bleeding through the sutures. He insisted we go right to the Therapist's office. He was so brave...so strong!

During the semester when I was studying Photography, he wanted to see what I was working on, as he was always interested in photography. I asked him at that time if I could go to the doctor with him on one of his visits and photograph him there. He was all over the idea and took me with him. He told the doctor that I'm his daughter and a grad student at the Art Institute of Chicago (he was so proud) and I'd be taking pictures. Now this is a man who's not at all revealing...very private—and here he is in his robe—so vulnerable. Anyway, I photographed all his scars. He had no problem with it...just said—"*do whatever you need to do* Jeanne."

You would think that over time and a succession of operations, anyone would become weaker and take longer to recover. Joe's first recovery period was about two months. After that, somehow he seemed to drastically shorten his recovery time. Following his first operation, Flo knew Joe would never slow down. Of course, this greatly concerned her. His remission would only last about two years but even at that time, the medical professionals told him his life expectancy was four years. Joe didn't buy it! He remained in a positive frame of mind and would often tell people that he didn't have cancer!

He didn't participate in chemotherapy. He knew that if something had to be removed, there was no other solution than surgery. But, he leaned heavily toward alternative therapies and Flo got busy in the research department.

He bought a 31 ft. RV motorhome to accommodate travel when he didn't feel well and they headed for Mexico to test the Gerson Therapy Program and nutritional supplements. Their longtime friend, Virginia

Hardy, remembers that Flo would never give up. Virginia said that "they both had the attitude that they'd do whatever was necessary. They went much farther than most people would have."

In an interview with *Motor Home Magazine*, Joe said "when I got home, I realized I couldn't go back to my office. I was actually captive to my house...like being a prisoner. I had to get out!" The motor home was transformed into an office that worked like a charm. It had a telephone, fax, typewriter and a full kitchen.

Joe did benefit from this juice therapy but it was oh-so-rigorous! The diet would test him continually. He always loved to cook...loved a variety of food—and now he's into organic foods, no sugar or fat. He had to use an electric juicer for fresh fruits and vegetables 13 times a day; this would test anyone's resolve! It became impossible to maintain without assistance. He hired Maria Johnson as his traveling assistant to prepare all of this for him. She rode along in the RV as Joe and Flo made his business calls.

Maria had been hired to prepare all Joe's special meals and juices. As Joe became more ill, Flo got much more involved in the business and of course, she had to travel with Joe. The juicing was intense. Check out the recipe for one of Joe's more frequent drinks: carrots, apples, olive juice, chard and liver. It did help and he felt better. Other ingredients for his delicious drinks included squash, kale and a variety of other less popular vegetables. It was working though! Maria said Joe and Flo treated her like family. She had come from Czechoslovakia and had a strong accent. She recalls: "When I go to interview, I was nervous but then I was comfortable, very good because he made a good thing to me. I liked him you know. She, too, very nice. Both was nice, very nice!"

The *cancer* word was rarely mentioned in the household or within the company. Everyone was pulling for Joe! His friends and business associates all wanted him to beat this hellacious nastiness that challenged him daily! Daughter Barb: "One evening before an operation the next day to remove 10 intestinal tumors, Dad was home reading the paper and I said "Dad, I'm worried about the operation." (This would be operation #16.) Joe looked up from his paper and said "Anna (he called Barb 'Anna'), I don't have cancer." Barb said, "OK Dad" and walked away stunned…shaking her head and laughing. But she isolated herself and broke down crying.

When Joe came out of this one, Barb was in the hall as they brought him down on the gurney and told Joe, "They got all ten of the tumors...they got 'em all out, Dad." Joe said "You're kidding me! Thank you Jesus!" And as they continued wheeling him down to intensive care, he continued: "Thank you, Jesus, thank you!" Joe hated the hospital and always wanted out as soon as possible. This may have made a positive contribution to his early recoveries.

Flo remembers: "Late into Joe's illness, we were approached by the company Super Cuts, who wanted to propose a purchase offer for The Barbers organization. There had been some earlier discussion and negotiation, but we turned their $3 million offer down. In the meantime, Joe went in for yet another operation. It didn't go well, in fact to top it off—he had an allergic reaction to the anesthesia. They rolled him up to intensive care and while I was sitting there with him, the phone rang...it was Super Cuts. He insisted on taking the call—you just couldn't slow the man down. Well, now they offered him $11 million for the company. He said he'd consider it and get back to them. After he hung up, I said "Joe—no possible way. You worked so hard for so long to build this company. No way will you sell if for $11 million!" Of course, they didn't sell to Super Cuts and they'd never regret it.

"In 1963, we risked it all, signed a lease for space that required us to pay more rent per month than we ever dreamed of making. We signed for a loan, put up all our furniture and car for the collateral. Fortunately, the bank didn't know the furniture was from the Salvation Army and the car was a $50.00 'junker.' We opened on a shoestring!"

John Reynolds: "Joe Francis once told me franchising allowed him to go into business for himself, but more important than that, it allowed him to go into business for his franchisees. His goal, to help others be successful and get a piece of the American Dream, created a corporate culture that really became a family. He'd give you the shirt off his back; he was that kind of a person."

Cheryl Babcock: "I took many groups of students and delegates from the U.S., England, Australia, Russia, and Siberia to tour The Barbers World Headquarters. Joe was a very effective educator and people were drawn to him. Perhaps because he came from the school of hard knocks, he could relate to anyone and inspire them by showing he wasn't afraid to try anything. I feel truly blessed to have had Joe in my life and to have been able to introduce him to so many people that benefited from the interaction."

John Paul DeJoria: "I would say Joe Francis was, beyond any question of doubt, a pioneer in the hair care industry and a brilliant leader. And his wife is super-duper, what a positive lady. Flo and Joe made you feel special, they listened to what you said as if you were the only person in the world that mattered."

Peggy (Scrappy) Schmidt: "I didn't always agree with him and what he did but I loved him. He taught me to respect and have confidence in myself. He taught me to love myself and gave me all the opportunity in the world. He used to tell me I should have it all...all the things I used to think were out of reach for me."

Dan Gallagher: "I think one of the greatest things I've ever seen, and it still chokes me up to think about it, was my 50th Birthday party. Joe and Flo were invited but I knew he was sick and probably wouldn't make it. Anyway, at the party, here comes Joe...right out of the hospital and he's wheelin' this thing with an intravenous bottle and IV needle in his arm. He and Flo came from the hospital wheeling this damn thing...it was truly something—unbelievable! Here's a man that's dying, (he's) in the hospital and he still finds a way to come see a friend at a birthday party. Joe, being an old fashioned family guy...I mean that's just how he was—wouldn't miss seeing me on my birthday. It was the most dramatic gesture I'd ever seen in my life!"

Dan, a retired Judge; and his wife Grace, are close personal friends of the Francis family.

Rocco Altobelli: "Joe really deserves a place in history, more than anyone in our business, because Joe really changed the industry."

Michael Cole: "Years after Joe passed, I'm at a Florida speaking engagement and afterwards, a woman from the audience comes up, introduces herself and tells me she was Joe's last assistant. She said "I understand you knew Joe Francis. I always wanted to come and hear you talk because Joe spoke so highly of you. He said if I ever had an opportunity to listen to you—I really had to do it. As a matter of fact, I was with Joe the day he got your last letter." She said that "as he read it, he kept telling her how great you are and what you achieved." I mean, what this lady said just gave me goose bumps because she remembered excerpts from my letter to Joe.

In essence, what I wrote was: Blessed are we, the chosen few, to have met someone as good as you. You helped us see in ourselves what we couldn't see and to develop it into an ability to use, that allowed us to leave the world better than we found it. I'll be forever grateful to you, Joe Francis. I'll see you on the other side; God speed you my friend.

"It's an honor and a sacred stewardship to keep his legacy, to deepen and expand and to bring to the world what he did. So a lot of times, if another mentor has passed something on to me that is useful, I'll speak about it in 'Joe Francis language'. Joe has become the metaphorical mentor because Joe was the catalyst. He was my first mentor and he taught me how to learn."

Franchisee Ruth Stadther: "When my husband, Lee, was sick with cancer, we had to sell our two salons back to the company. I was Lee's primary caregiver, he was ill and we just couldn't run them. When Lee died, I realized I wanted to get back to work and I asked Joe if he'd sell the salons back to me. This was a big problem for the company because they had already sold the salons to new Franchisees. Joe had to negotiate for me and talk the new owners into selling back to me. He became my number one supporter and mentor."

Within 18 months, Ruth had two more salons and all her locations were profitable. In the process, while she was testing her wings, Ruth frequently called Joe for help and advice. "Joe made himself available on a daily basis, even though he was in and out of the hospital. He never gave an indication of how sick he really was...never complained nor talked about what he was going through. The same was true for Flo; they were both strong people who always had time for you regardless of what was going on in their lives. It was absolutely amazing."

Dale Loucks, Award-winning stylist and Franchisee: "We loved the competitive events. Aside from all the awards I had won, my two daughters, Angie and Nikki, also won many awards. We were in St. Paul at an event and Joe was there with his friend from Japan. Joe didn't look good and I offered to help him get to his car. He was really sick but wanted to be at this competition. Three days later, Joe died during his last surgery."

Norm Stoehr, Business partner-Entrepreneur: "Joe going through an operation was like the average person with a cold. That's how he approached it. He never seemed to see it as a life or death situation. He saw it as an inconvenience. He just blew me away. Joe told me once that he was trying to talk the doctors into velcroing him...so they wouldn't have to keep cutting him open. I don't know how he could joke about it. He was often back to work the next day or at least on the phone... unbelievable!"

Susan Goldstein, Joe's daughter: "I remember the Sunday before my Dad died we went to church together at St. John's in Little Canada. He couldn't walk very well anymore, so he had a handicapped sticker on his car. We parked in a spot right next to the door, where we could walk in directly to the front pew. We sat there and I was crying the whole time because I knew it might be the last time I'd be with my dad at church. I cried through the whole service...couldn't stand or kneel...just sat there sobbing with Dad holding my hand. The priest came over to us at communion because he knew my dad couldn't walk up there.

"When we were driving home, I said 'Dad, I'm sorry.' And he said, 'No, it's OK, Sue.' At the house we all sat down in the solarium and I said, 'Dad, we have to talk about your funeral.' I knew the church was important to him and we just had to do this. Mom suggested having Robert Robinson, a gospel singer in the Twin Cities, sing. My Dad thought that would be nice. We were all there for this—me, Barb, Jeanne, Johnny and Joey. We had to cry and talk about it."

Joe would go in for his final surgery the next day.

When Joe's Japanese friend, Tak Nomoto learned of Joe's illness, he was very concerned. There's a Japanese legend that if one folds (Origami) a thousand cranes, it so pleases the gods that the person folding is granted a wish. Tak and family folded the thousand cranes to form a *Senba-Zuru* and sent them to Joe. The wish that Tak made was for Joe's recovery.

When Flo wrote back to thank him, she told him they had it hanging over their bed. After Joe's passing, Tak wrote this letter to Flo:

> Since I met Joe on Independence Day at the American Centennial celebration, he and Florence have become rare friends of our family. In spite of the fact that we live in opposite places on this earth, such a long acquaintance is nothing but destiny and fortune favoring me. Mr. Joseph Francis and Mrs. Florence Francis are my family's rare friends. Mr. Joseph Francis is a great man and treats all who he comes into contact with, in love, tolerance and intimacy. I'll never forget him and will often be reminded of his affectionate smile. Thank you again Mr. Joseph Francis and Mrs. Florence Francis and your family. We will stay friends a long time.
>
> Tak and family

Jeff Roberts—fellow entreprenuer and friend: Joe had come to see me about a week before his last surgery. He told me it was, at best, only a 50/50 chance he'd make it. He was really in bad shape and hurting all the time...the internal bleeding and all. He said he wanted me to know he loved me. He came to see me to tell me that. So, when I got the call about him passing...I think it was Flo that called...I can't even remember; I was in shock. And Joe's funeral at St. John's church in Little Canada...I mean it was like the Head of State passed... talk about packed! *(There was standing room only. It's estimated there were over 1,500 people in attendance.)* I don't remember how many people gave eulogies but the service was just fabulous! Police had to direct traffic, which was jammed for blocks around.

Afterward, Flo had a get-together at their house on the lake and it was absolutely upbeat. Just a loving enjoyable afternoon, because Joe's passing was expected and people seemed to be ready for it. All those expressions of grief turned to expressions of joy. It wasn't like the atmosphere after most funerals, it was really nice."

John Francis: "Dad, Mom and I were in Las Vegas for an IFA convention in February of 1994. Dad should not have been traveling, he was so sick. We had to bring his whole medical file with us on the chance that if he was in trouble, we'd have all the pertinent information. He loved the IFA conventions and just insisted that we go. I had taken in some workshops and the three of us planned to meet back in the convention hall later and go to dinner. When I got back, I couldn't find them anywhere. Turned out he was in the hospital. He had started bleeding internally again and was in Emergency getting a transfusion.

Sad as it was at the time, I became very angry with him...about how we never should have come here and that we should have stayed home. I reacted to fear with anger. The doctors told us they couldn't release him; that if they did, he surely would die within a matter of hours. They were frantically trying to find a medical emergency airplane to fly him to Mayo Clinic in Rochester, Minnesota. One of the IFA attendees, a man named Loren Steele, who owned the Super 8 Hotel franchise, learned about our dilemma. He had his own private jet and offered to fly us home. But Dad found out that we could take a commercial flight and wanted to take that instead...I'm sure he didn't want Loren to be put out.

When we landed in Minneapolis, a pre-arranged ambulance was on the runway. They took him off first and Mom jumped into the ambulance as it sped off for Mayo Clinic. I collected all our bags, ran them home and then took off for Rochester. Somehow, he pulled out of this one too.

But, within a month we were back at the Clinic. His digestive tract was perforated with tumors and he was bleeding into himself. They can transfuse but you can't live with new blood coming through you all the time. They had to operate. They gave him a 20% chance to survive. We were all in his room prior to the surgery; they expected the surgery prep would take an hour or so. We were riding the elevator with him and he told us: "Get some breakfast, eat something good for me." We had been up all night with Dad and everyone was really exhausted. We're in the waiting room later—Mom, Sadie, his mother, and lots of grandkids too. A nurse came down and told us to follow her. As we walked quickly to the area, tears streamed down our faces. We went down to a small room next to the Surgery facility and the doctor came out. He looked at us and said, "Joe is no longer with us. (We were all frozen with grief.) His blood pressure dropped off the charts and his heart gave out. We revived him but he went into Cardiac arrest and we lost him."

We went in to see him and everyone broke down. Sadie, his mother, was wailing. We were all crying... there's just no way to prepare for something like this. (Later, Mom took his wedding band off and kept it until I got married. She gave it to me for *my* wedding band.) We started making calls. It was so sad, so hard, to tell everyone. We all went back to Mom and Dad's house."

They were all together and Flo came out of Joe's office with a notebook pad of letters Joe had handwritten. She told us that Joe, in anticipation of passing, had written a farewell letter to each his children.

(Author note:) But Flo didn't get a personal letter. Those who were closest to Joe have a theory about this. Flo was his girlfriend, his wife, his strength, his children's mother, his grandchildren's "Nana." How—how could Joe bring himself to say goodbye to his sweetheart? 'Goodbye' to Flo? 'Goodbye' to this grand lady who was always there for him? He probably *tried* to write a goodbye to Flo many times over. He probably choked and became so morose in the process, he just couldn't get it done. He did write a letter to Flo and their children (in addition to the individual letters to each of his five children) in which he wrote of Flo in great detail. But then, Joe knew that Flo was aware that she was his world. Flo, more than anyone or thing, had been his inspiration to succeed. If there was ever a person he wanted to be proud of him, it was his wife, Flo.

A Champion to the very end, Joe Francis wasn't thinking about himself.

Ralph Waldo Emerson wrote: "Men of character are the conscience of the society to which they belong." *(A good description of Joe Francis.)*

A man with a loving heart will most likely be a man of manners. All who would come into contact with Joe Francis would see both qualities within this man. You could see it in his eyes. He had a lot of eye glitter...a personal trait found in most successful people. In Joe, it was a trait that rose to a crescendo of a *twinkle* when he was excited about an idea; or when he listened to someone telling him about their ambitions, aspirations and plans. And, that twinkle was always there when he talked about his business or his family.

Joe Francis had a loving heart. While he could tolerate bad language in others, the number of cuss words that ever came from Joe's mouth could probably be counted on one hand. So many people we talked with about the man would say they never heard him raise his voice or use "blue" language. Joe Francis was a consummmate gentleman. Humility requires courage, something this soft-spoken, warm-hearted man had in abundance. He had a tolerance level few could ever match. These character traits served Joe well in all negotiating matters. Even if he did something that would irritate others, they found it hard to stay annoyed with him. All of the people we talked with, who had employment interviews with Joe, echoed similar stories; since his success and reputation preceded him, they would often feel intimidated or nervous coming in to see him. But, to a person, they all said that within seconds to minutes, he put them completely at ease. Not really surprising, since Joe always had a profound interest in the happiness and success of others. Seems he wanted everyone to win—and to win big! He was just as willing to let you know about his failures or shortcomings as he was to talk about his successes. No wonder then, that people were quickly drawn to Joe Francis. He never represented a threat...always a safe harbor. He was always an impassioned listener...always encouraging his family, friends and associates.

Joe Francis was a hard act to follow. His associate, Richard King, said: "Joe Francis is a man I truly respected because I never saw him cut people up. I have worked in corporations where that's typical but I think Joe's approach was one that always gathered people together."

Shortly after Joe passed, his daughter Jeanne was going through his desk drawers at the Francis home. When she opened two large drawers, she discovered one was full of business cards—all helter skelter, and the other full of pink 'While You Were Out' telephone message slips. As she went through the message slips, she found they dated back six years. This gave her the inspiration to have her dad help her with her graduate school final artwork project.

Jeanne put the messages in chronological order by date and then pinned them to the walls. They covered all four walls of a room eight feet square, from floor to ceiling. She then took all the business cards and put them in spiral fashion on the floor in the middle of the room. Next, she set up seven tape recorders with speakers and concealed them behind the walls. The tape recordings were to summon the attention of any visitor to the room regarding Joe's whirlwind business. She titled her project "While You Were Out"; she said it was her "bittersweet success."

Joe was gone now, on to his next great adventure. He had brought the company to a place that offered monumental potential. While there was yet much to be accomplished, he had surrounded Flo with competent counsel and expertise throughout his staff and the Board of Directors. Now, in the shadow of Joe's spirit, goes Flo...she's determined that this company will grow and continue to lead the industry.

Joe had expected to leave Flo with substantial life insurance proceeds. Bad news though...one of his policies worth $1,000,000 had lapsed. This was a policy that had been set up for the company to pay the premium. How it lapsed, no one knew, but this was a shock to Flo.

Next, Flo was faced with repaying the company for loans Joe had taken out. These totaled more than a million dollars. What a rolling start; losing Joe, a family debt problem and a large debt obligation to The Barbers. Nevertheless, Flo would prove she was up for this challenge.

CHAPTER 13

IN THE SHADOW

The Barbers 1994 National Convention had been planned for a long time. No one knew it would take place in late April, 1994, just two weeks after Joe died. Flo was not ready to attend and no one expected her to be there. She couldn't sleep the night before the opening day of the convention. Flo realized she had a leadership role to fulfill. She felt a deep obligation to go tell all the company staff and franchisees that they would be "OK"; the company would not fall apart. She began writing a speech and would continue to write and rewrite until 7:00 a.m. When Flo came walking into the convention that morning, few could believe their eyes.

The Barbers National Convention
Flo Francis presiding:

> "Good Morning! It's good to see all of you! Welcome to Minneapolis.
>
> I'd like to thank all of you for your sympathy. Losing Joe is a terrible thing. My family and I are still in the midst of grief and it helps to know that so many others are also grieving for Joe. Some of you have been with the company for twenty—even thirty years. You're like family—Earl, Gil, Charlie, Dale, Marv, Bill, Pete, Gary, Jim, Bob, Don, Ruth, Susie, Joe, Walt, Ron, Doug, Dave, Bertil, Dick—
>
> We know that you share our pain and realize that Joe's passing is truly the great loss we feel it is.
>
> Joe worked long and hard for this company. Joe poured his life into this company, right up to the very end.
>
> Joe's dream was shared by so many and I want to see his dream live on.
>
> For the past 12 years, Joe had 23 cancer surgeries. He never let his illness stop him or even slow him down! Joe was very courageous. He fought a long, hard fight to build this company and conquer cancer. He fought with passion;

he worked, toiled, suffered, and lived life fully—every day of his life!

Joe and I knew this day would come. We planned the transition. We talked to the Board of Directors, we talked to Fred. I have taken Joe's job and Joe's title but I can never take his place. No one could. But I want to keep his spirit alive, his love for this business; his devotion to this company; and his joy in your success!

I am as dedicated as Joe to keep this company strong and growing. I will do everything in my power to improve our image, our profitability and our success and effectiveness.

The people I have to work with are the best. Our Board of Directors and Corporate Management have never been stronger. Our Board has committed themselves to long-term strategic goals that will ensure our careful growth and success. Fred and I are committed to each other and this company. Fred has been very supportive of me in Joe's absences and we plan to carry on—with no changes. I'm not going to bow out! I'm going to stay and run the company—just as we have been.

Joe did all the hard work. We have everything we need for continued success. But you are the

> heart of this company! You are the glue that holds this company together.
>
> In 1982 we had four Cost Cutters. In 1983, Joe lost a kidney to cancer. In the next 11 years, we built 650 Cost Cutters and Joe had over 20 major surgeries. And it was a hard 11 years! I look forward to the next 11 years, with hundreds or thousands of more salons and no surgeries.
>
> I intend to continue Joe's work. I want to run a very professional, serious and conservative company...because that's the way it has to be run! I intend to make you proud to be professionally associated with me...as I am proud to be associated with you!
>
> You mean a lot to me! You meant a lot to Joe! Let's keep going! Let's do it for Joe!"

The standing ovation would become a prelude to more and better things to come. And, no doubt, Joe Francis was in attendance...stood first, clapped loudest and sat down last. His sweetheart was at the helm and this time, the powerful ocean liner had a rudder.

After Flo's address, franchisees gathered around her. They told her that what she had said was exactly what they wanted to and needed to hear. They would rally around her. The Barber's corporate attorney, John Fitzgerald, said: "Flo didn't just hand off the baton to Fred Huggins. Her presence at the convention was essential. It conveyed to the Franchisees that they would have the Francis family presence, even though Joe was gone."

Flo knew the business and had an intense and extraordinary focus on the management end of things. She asked tough questions and wanted answers at the Board meetings. Flo, at age 57, was stepping up to the plate. Her proactive approach to matters and inordinate work ethic was evident. She wasn't watching the clock, she was watching the helm. Fred Huggins said "Flo is at the office every morning by 8:00 a.m. and is the last to leave in the evening." He liked her conservative view and the fact that she stuck to the company's strategic plan; he felt that Flo was tremendously intuitive and sharp. She quickly earned the respect of Board members, Staff and Franchisees, as the company moved forward.

Longtime friend and business associate, JoAnne Shaw, owner of The Coffee Beanery, knew Joe as a warm, caring individual determined to accomplish great things. And, she also knew Flo as a vibrant, exciting person to be around and a very capable businesswoman...one who was astute and had the leadership skills to take over for Joe.

Flo remembers some Board meetings when the "B" word, (bankruptcy) was mentioned. Even though company-wide sales were rocketing, the company bottom line needed help. Now, more than ever before, Flo could see that getting on the big board of NASDAQ would be the answer.

If anyone knew how to operate on a thin budget, it was Flo! She had done it for years with their family budget, as her loving husband had schooled her in "Life Lesson 101"; how to get by on a little and be in-the-dark while doing it. She had no trouble teaming up with Fred and following a strategic plan. With their noses to the grindstone, they increased net income by 40%...quite an achievement, when system sales grew by only 6%!

Flo wrote in the 1994 annual report: "As a company, we remain dedicated to the success of our franchisees and to continuing to enhance the value of our shareholders' investments in The Barbers. The future is bright and we look forward to reporting to you on our progress."

When the books were closed on 1995, there was much good news. Through diligent efforts to grow and still control spending, the management team was sparkling. Net income had grown by 37% over the previous year to $840,000—48 cents per share! The pursuit of NASDAQ was no longer a possibility...it was now a probability. The company was recognized that year at the national level. They were ranked #12 in the top U.S. Franchise Companies. (There were over 2,500 business format franchises in the U.S. at that time.)

Flo and Fred really had great respect for the talents and skills of each other. Flo knew Fred was a sharp and calculating businessman, who could talk the talk—and walk it too. Fred saw her as very controlled and street smart, a leader the franchisees would follow.

It was about this time that John Francis was looking for more responsibility. He got along great with Fred—and Fred respected John's work ethic and intellect. Fred thought it was time to further test John and give him his own projects, rather than have him assist others. Fred had a buy-out target in mind, a company called "We Care Hair." He told John he'd like him to take on the project. With this in mind, John attended an AMA 'Mergers and Acquisitions' Workshop in Chicago. This would be a large and challenging project. We Care Hair had about 150 salons. John is up for the challenge and digs in. He finds out that the franchisees for this company are nowhere as content as The Barbers franchisees. There are myriad problems—salons losing money, lack of support, lawsuits pending—a veritable mess! But In 1997 the acquisition successfully merged "We Care Hair" into The Barbers organization.

At the close of fiscal 1996, Flo Francis was happy to report the realization of a long-time goal.... The Barbers were now on the NASDAQ. They were now a public traded company. What an achievement—and that was only a portion of the good news. Earnings were up *again* by 26%...net income was over $1 million! And, there was more; they were nationally recognized again, as the #28 top U.S. franchise company and the *only* hair company in the top 100. Things were different! There was some money in the coffers...the "B" word went away.

1996 Convention
Flo Francis presiding

Two members of The Barbers Founders Club received special recognition at the year-end convention.

> "I now have the pleasure of presenting two Lifetime Achievement awards to members of the Founders Club, who have been with this company for at least 30 years! One of you has been with us for 39 years and the other for 31 years. They bore the brunt of those early years; when Joe started his mission in the '60s, and they were ready to do whatever they could to help Joe build his company. As Joe said many times... "I didn't do this alone."
>
> The first Lifetime Award goes to a man who has been with us for 31 years! He literally saved this company with sheer determination and dedication. This man was "farmed out" to nearly all our locations within the first few years, to teach customer service and product ideas. We needed his talent badly and had to spread him pretty thin in those days. He gave hundreds of classes at night and on weekends for many months. The business grew and he grew with us. Through it all, he has retained his ever-present sense of humor. That man is Earl Faulkner.

> Earl, I can't overstate the contribution you've made to this company. Earl, please come up and receive your Lifetime Achievement Award.
>
> The next Lifetime Award goes to a person who so richly deserves recognition for putting in *39* years of service. He literally grew up in the business and worked every aspect; from shining shoes and spreading door-to-door flyers as each shop opened, to sweeping floors and stocking shelves as a kid, then getting a business degree and advancing up the ladder through the company. Today, he's a franchisee who can say he's done it all! Joe and I have always been so proud of him and it's time we acknowledge his lifetime contribution. He is our son Joe. Joey...thanks for all you've done...come on up here!"

Quite a party...a spectacular year. System-wide sales were over $211 million and corporate net income over $1.8 million.

Everything was going in a positive direction; well, almost everything. Through her twelve years of nurturing, nursing and tending to Joe while he battled cancer and worked like a madman, Flo had neglected her own health. She was OK, but often pretty uncomfortable. Over the past couple years she had dealt with a back operation, bladder operation, a severely sprained ankle and a detached retina...all while at the helm of

The Barbers. Nevertheless, there was work to be done and Flo toiled on.

Then...in the spring of 1997, the worst nightmare any parent could imagine. Her firstborn son, Joey, lost his life in a tragic car accident. Not possible...just couldn't be true, but it was true. The loss of Joey within a few years of Joe's death was an impossible burden. This knocked Flo off her feet and months of depression followed. Not hard to understand her grief and anguish, not hard to empathize with this grand lady; how she pulled it back together is a wonderment. Flo said she came out of this dark place because of her love and concern for her four remaining children.

Joey's funeral was attended by over 1,000 people. His influence on co-workers, employees, friends and family was demonstrated that sad day in the Francis family history.

Mike Kampmeyer, Jr., a close friend of Joey, said that when he learned of Joey's passing, it was like being kicked in the stomach—"Joey was the kind of person you just expected to go on forever because of his energy and enthusiasm."

Joey was a handsome man with an infectious smile, eye glitter, sharp wit and a love for the family and company parties. He was at a point in life where he had decided on a new venture into other businesses and had planned to sell off his franchised salons. He looked forward to testing his own entrepreneurial bent but he never got the opportunity.

His brother, John, who had worked side by side with Joey through the years, said "Just as Joey was picking up new momentum, he died; it just didn't seem right."

Joey's sister, Susan, had helped him following their dad's passing, to manage the family owned Pennsylvania Cost Cutter salons and get them ready to sell. She had a family to care for as well, but this was a huge project...Joey needed help and Sue was there for him. She treasured the time they spent together.

His sister Jeanne felt that his death brought the family even closer. They placed Joey next to his dad at Riverview Memorial Cemetery in West St. Paul. In the obituary, the family asked that any memorials be sent to the Joe Francis Scholarship Foundation. Over $15,000 was donated...more testimony to Joey's influence on friends and associates. The haunting reverie, though, will never go away.

Flo's strong faith had lifted her up once more. She took some solace in the thought that Joey was in a good place and once again, with his dad. Flo would just have to keep on moving on, and as difficult as it was, she did move on...continuing to build The Barbers. With the acquisition of We Care Hair, they closed 1997 with 935 salons and sales up 19.5 per cent.

More impressive yet, was that net income had increased to $1.4 million and return on shareholders' equity was 22.7%. They were keeping up on the service end for franchises as well. Staff was added, services expanded and "Franchise Gold" magazine rated them #10 of all U.S. franchise companies with 500-1,000 units. "Franchise Times" magazine ranked them #11 of the *top 200* franchise companies and #2 in health and personal care. In addition, they were ranked #2 in the top 200 for training and support to franchisees. These rankings were in league with such heavyweights as McDonalds.

If only Joe Francis could have been there. He was always so big on training, so big on service. Joe had predicted years prior, that more women would become managers and franchise owners. There was more publicity as "Opportunities" magazine rated The Barbers as one of the *top* franchise companies in America. They were also recognized as the #1 company in Minnesota's 200 largest publicly traded companies, for having the highest percentage of women in top management. Eight of their top seventeen officers were women. Joe had called it again.

At the year-end company convention, Flo gave this heart wrenching tribute to her son, Joey: "It is with the deepest sadness I have ever known that I tell you this: the unthinkable and impossible has happened. My dear son, Joey, died March 9th."

The outpouring of sympathy from the people of this company when he died was overwhelming—the flowers, cards and letters. When Joey died, you were all so good to us. Your immediate response to his death was just as it was when Joe died. You gave us such strong support—it really helped us. We will never be the same without Joey, but you have helped us again and we thank you.

What a great example of this company's heart! As his mother, along with his brother, sisters and his children, I want to thank you for paying such a great tribute to my son. We will never stop missing him and we will never be the same without him. Death certainly changes a relationship but it doesn't end. I still have a relationship with Joey. I feel very close to him. He still has an influence on my life...on all our lives. The impact he had on us while he was alive will never end.

Joey was first and foremost a good Dad. He had five children, whom he was devoted to. Two of his children are here tonight. Would you stand up? Benji, his oldest son is 12 and Monica, his oldest daughter—9. His three other little ones are at home.

Joey received the Lifetime Achievement Award at last November's convention. His story, in his own words, can be found in the Founders Club Book. He started working at The Barbers, like his dad—as a shoeshine boy—when he was only 8. He was so proud of our company and did anything we needed done: cleaning, painting, delivering supplies and later with a marketing degree, he worked in the home office, and lastly as a franchisee. Joey's contribution to this company was tremendous.

Just like his Dad, more than anyone else, Joey wanted this company to succeed! As the company grew, he was overjoyed.

Losing Joe and now Joey has been the biggest challenge our family will ever face. We will never be the same. But we'll get through this and be closer than ever.

Because there's nothing we can't deal with now. And we know what's important—it is family. And this year I am so lucky to have my family here with me—my daughter Susan, her husband Jeff and my 3 grandchildren, Rachel, Adam and Sarah, two of my son Joey's children; Benji and Monica and their mother Margaret and her husband Wade, my daughters Barb and Jeanne and my son John.

Life is precious and fleeting—it should be simplified to what matters most—work is important but family has to be number one priority."

The Barbers ended their 35th year in 1998. Wow... what a year! *Nations Business* magazine touted The Barbers as one of only seven franchises featured. They were seen as a franchise organization with all the ingredients *to become a legend*. They had concept, vision, talent, enthusiasm and ability. Publicity like this is pure gold.

It keeps coming...*Forbes* magazine: "One of the 200 best overall companies in the U.S.," (based on the toughest screening in 20 years). They looked at sales growth, earnings, return on equity and required that the company exceed a 20% return on earnings for five successive years. *Success* magazine: "One of the top 100 franchise companies in the U.S." *Venture* magazine: "One of the six most successful businesses in Minnesota." *Corporate Report*: "Rated #11 of the 20 best growing companies in Minnesota." And, a very big player in the industry is watching.

The company's convention was held in Acapulco and it was more than just special or memorable; it was on a near-spiritual level. Flo had published The Founder's Club book and said: "This is a permanent record and priceless historical reference this company will cherish for years to come. She was paying homage to Joe's early, loyal and loving troops, The Barbers Founders. All had been with The Barbers through every nightmare they endured. All had gone far past the extra mile. Here's Flo's speech at the convention:

"I want to acknowledge and honor 35 people...the people who built this company and made it what it is today. The number 35 may be small when compared to our total number of 300 plus franchisees, but these 35 people are majestic in our eyes!

These people gambled, along with Joe and I, that The Barbers Corporation would succeed...and they were right! When we began to franchise The Barbers' salons in 1970, it took more than cash, time and energy to get things off the ground. It took guts and blind faith in Joe's dream. These people believed in Joe's dream.

To honor these pioneers, we have established the *Founders Club*...an elite group of people who have been with us for at least 20 years and are still working with The Barbers Corporation. We have their names on this official Founders Club plaque, which will be on permanent display in the lobby of our headquarters.

In addition, each of these people was asked to provide, in their own words, a biography. We've compiled those that were submitted and had them bound as *The Founders Club* book for their memory box.

I can't tell you how much these personal stories mean to me and my family. They tell it all exactly as it happened, how their lives changed and how they felt along the way. Sincere and honest accounts of how they related to Joe and he to them...reading them has touched me deeply. Their experiences are now a permanent record and priceless historical reference that this company will cherish for years to come.

Many of you Founders are here tonight. I'd like to introduce you, so please stand as I read each name and remain standing until I finish. You all stood by Joe through thick and thin. Thank you, my friends. I thank you and my family thanks you and Joe thanks you. Please see me immediately after the awards, to receive your book and certificate and pose for a group picture.

I can't forget those who worked with us who are no longer here. We must always remember Lee Stadther, Jim Morehouse, Jerry Vanetta, Bob Miller and Marv Alvheim. Also, I want to especially acknowledge Dale Horsfield. Could you please stand. Dale, who's retiring this year, for the first time in 21 years will not be a franchisee. Thank you Dale, for all your years. Your contribution to the company and mutual memories will never be forgotten.

"Our Founders then: Bertil Anderberg, Doug Barnes, Ron Battern, Donald Bohn, Hob Breeze, Charles Brown, Gary Clausen, Jim Curran, Richard Davidson, James Grady, Earl Faulkner, Walt Freiberg, Everal Gilbertson, Vikki Hahn, Doug & Linda Hill, Gary Heskin, Dick Johnson, Bill Kaminski, Dale & Jean

Loucks, Joe & Vernice McCullough, Tom Mumaw, Dennis Peterson, Cherie Ross, Ruth Stadther, Bob Thorpe, Don & Deb Thorpe, Joseph Francis Sr., Myself-Flo Francis, Joseph Francis Jr., Tracy Fritz, Dale Horsefield, Patty Kessler."

One of the Founders Club earliest members, Charlie Brown, wrote to Flo in 1998, "This company becomes a lifestyle, not just an ownership in a number of salons. The people within the company become a family, and this family has endured the greatest test; the test of time."

One more important event took place in 1998. Joe Francis would no doubt have been ever so proud and happy for his colleague, Bill Kaminski. Bill was chosen as the 1998 Franchisee of the Year, by the International Franchise Association (IFA). Back in 1969, while a very young man just getting off the ground during his first 30 days with The Barbers, Bill had won first place, as an apprentice, at the Upper Midwest Barbers Association competition. And now, this ultimate recognition; both he and Joe were recipients of this prestigious award.

CHAPTER 14

WHO'S THAT KNOCKING?

The company continued to grow and a huge competitor, Regis Salons, was not only watching, they were making inquiries about buying The Barbers. John Francis was impressed with the Regis organization. Flo and John discussed the idea to consider selling to Regis. Flo had worked so hard, for so long and the idea of retirement was somewhat inviting. But she was concerned about John's future. John was all for selling, provided they got the offer they deserved. He saw a merger with Regis to be best for everyone. They were based locally and planned to keep everyone but the top officers, who would retire gracefully. Five consecutive years of net income growth exceeding 25% per year, 980 salons up and running and system sales exceeding $211 million...the time was right.

Flo, however, wanted to see the company attain the 1,000 salon mark in 1999. In the early months of that year, The Barbers opened a new and much larger—beauty product and supplies distribution center. From this new 20,000 square foot facility, they could ship product within a 24-48 hour timeline. Additional improvements in their distribution efficiency were helping to increase cash flow.

The year was bringing more valuable publicity via media accolades as well. *Entrepreneur* magazine rated the Cost Cutters in the top 500 women-owned businesses in the United States. *Working Woman* magazine listed Flo and The Barbers #383 among the nation's top 500 women-based businesses, right in the mix with Martha Stewart, Donna Karan and Leone Helmsley. *City Business* magazine ranked The Barbers #10 in largest franchise store revenues. But the greatest of awards and recognition came from the International Franchise Association. In 1999, they honored Joe and Flo Francis by inducting them into the IFA Hall of Fame. They were recognized as franchise leadership icons, along with many other legendary leaders, such as Ray Kroc of McDonalds, Colonel Saunders of Kentucky Fried Chicken, and William Rosenberg of Dunkin' Donuts.

Regis was still at the door and making offers...what to do? This was an emotional roller coaster period for Flo. To think The Barbers would be no more, to recall the toil, anguish, hard work, blood and tears...is it time to let go? On the other hand, if they sold to Regis, The Barbers would land in good hands and continue to grow.

For Flo, thinking about how she and Joe had sacrificed so much, put so much of their lives into the business, worked countless hours; she couldn't help but ponder the luxury of retirement. If only Joe could be here, she thought. He lived so big, had such a good time, he'd be "tap dancing" for the rest of his life. It *was* the right thing to do. Flo thought ahead...to have financial stability would be a new experience. She said to a friend: "I won't know how to act...I'll still feel like I'm overdrawn at the bank."

In May of 1999, the deal came to fruition and the two largest, publicly traded companies in the hair salon industry were now one; bringing to a close the 36 years of operation of "The Barbers." The franchisees now continued on in business as a part of Regis.

For The Barbers shareholders it was a $58.7 million deal. Flo remembered that back in 1994, Joe had often told her that she didn't need to worry. He'd said, that even if he died, the company would prosper and she'd be financially secure. The two companies had salons in 510 Wal-Mart locations and were opening about 120 per year between them. The Cost Cutters-Wal-Mart relationship had been the biggest attraction in the deal for Regis.

Five years after the merger, CEO Paul Finkelstein was quoted in the local paper (June 6, 2004 St. Paul Pioneer Press): "Regis' arrangement with Wal-Mart has blossomed into a growth center beyond our wildest dreams." He went on to forecast that in 2005, his company expected to hit the $400 million mark in sales from 1,500 salons in Wal-Mart.

Reaching back to that day on Joe's deck...at his home on the lake, to the discussion about whether to consider a low cost concept (Cost Cutters), it could have been different...but it wasn't.

From Joe's unique involvement in Russia, to John's resolute efforts to bring in that deal...it could have been different...but it wasn't. Connecting in France, hooking up with Wal-Mart...it could have been different...but it wasn't. Joe's vision, intuition, persistence and risk taking had all paid off.

Some of the franchisees were in shock when they got the news. Would this be a positive change for them? Regis is a large and professional organization run by highly skilled and talented people. One of the most compelling reasons for Flo to merge with them was that the oldest franchisees wanted to retire and Regis was willing to buy them out for a very good price. This was an excellent way for these franchisees to exit. In addition, Regis would nurture and help integrate those franchisees who continued in business. It was a win-win plan for everyone.

Joe Francis was determined to reach his goals, to make poor men rich, to leave his family with wealth; to make certain his life's love, Flo Francis, was out of harm's way and in the clover. Joe had been gone since 1994 and much of the success of the company came later. However, ideas are nothing without someone acting on them. Dreams are just that unless someone makes them real.

Joe Francis didn't live in the land of 'coulda, woulda, shoulda'! Joe was the epitome of ideas in motion, of leading by example, of a sincere interest in the well being of others, of taking calculated risks. He just plain got it done! Those who followed early and close behind, those loyal men and women, the "Founders Club" members; the franchisees; Joe's family, all would benefit tremendously for taking this trip from Mazeppa to Moscow and back!

The spirit of Joe Francis surrounds them. He would glow with pride and be forever grateful for the success and happiness of this huge, loving family, The Barbers.

CHAPTER 15

THE AFTERGLOW

Joe's spirit lives on in grand style through the Joe Francis Scholarship Foundation. The goal is to build the Foundation to a place were its perpetuity is guaranteed. Contributions are appreciated by both the Foundation and the recipients and can be sent to: P.O. Box 50625, Minneapolis, MN 55405

John Francis established the "Post Net" franchises, as area developer, for all of Minnesota and Wisconsin. John received Post Net's "Franchisee of the Year" in 2007.

John also serves on the Board of the International Franchise Association, the third member in the Francis family to do so. John received the IFA's "Franchisee of the Year" in 2008. John and his wife Jennell have two daughters, Lilly and Anna, and live in St. Paul, MN.

Barb Francis enjoys her role as President of the Joe Francis Scholarship Foundation (JFSF) and working with Flo, who is the Chairman of the board. Barb is a Group Life Counselor at a residential treatment center in Washington state, working with teenage girls who are addicted to drugs or alcohol.

Jeanne Francis Dietrich is on the Board of the JFSF, working with her sister, Barb, and Flo. She is active in the arts and interior design and belongs to Norm Stoehr's "Inner Circle" group of entrepreneurs. Jeanne has a six-year-old son, Joseph Francis Dietrich.

Susan Goldstein is happily retired from her position on the Board of The Barbers and past president of the JFSF. She volunteers at Hennepin county Medical Center. Susan and her husband Jeff have three children, Rachel, Adam and Sarah.

Joey, who died suddenly at the age of 39, in a car accident, left five children; Benjamin, Monica, Andrew, Brianna and Joseph.

Flo finds time to travel and visit her many friends in the United States, France and elsewhere. On Joe's birthday in 1998, she purchased a log home on a beautiful lake in northern Wisconsin. She named it "Camp Joseph." All of her children and the grandkids love to visit there. The playhouse Joe had built for the grandkids many years earlier, was so loved that Flo had it duplicated at Camp Joseph for their grandchildren; Joseph, Lilly and Anna, who were born after Joe's passing.

Flo was totally surprised by her children on her 70th birthday. Her children held an elaborate party for her that included a Master of Ceremony, entertainment and music. They said they wanted to do it this way because that's the way Joe would have done it.

The Francis family is and remains very close and all are supportive of each other...something Joe would expect and appreciate.

CHAPTER 16

THANKS FOR THE ROSES

Joe's company received a huge amount of recognition, awards and accolades from many different sources. His personal accomplishments, spread out over many years, had earned him more awards than anyone else in his business. Always known as a man of integrity, he cared greatly for colleagues, staff and franchisees; it's no wonder that *The Barbers never had a lawsuit filed against them in 36 years of operation.*

In 1999, Joe and Flo Francis were inducted into the prestigious International Franchise Association Hall of Fame.

The IFA is based in Washington, D.C., with a staff of lawyers, marketing and public relations specialists. Their main purpose is to service the IFA Board of Directors, and facilitate the local, regional, national and international meetings of this Board, as well as the annual International Convention, which is at the direction of the Board.

This award, IFA's oldest and most prestigious, is presented to an IFA member, past or present, who exemplifies the optimum in franchising and has contributed significantly to the advancement of franchising and the franchising community. The Hall of Fame Award is a limited edition porcelain eagle with outstretched wings, produced by Boehm, whose porcelains are on permanent exhibit in The Metropolitan Museum of Art, the Vatican, Buckingham Palace, the Hermitage, the Smithsonian and other museums throughout the world. The eagle was selected for this IFA award because it symbolizes the strength, power and independence of the entrepreneurial spirit, intrinsic to franchising.

From the most humble beginnings as Minnesota's youngest barber at age 17, to an international franchise organization that would promote and lead the beauty industry...that is the history of The Barbers. Founders Joe and Florence Francis spent their adult lives bringing an American dream to fruition and in the process, left a legacy for their children, the beauty industry and franchising.

Joe's dreams, visions and actions were fueled by powerful forces: a love affair with life and his sweetheart and stalwart wife. In the 36 years since the founding of The Barbers, change has been a constant, from setting up the Midwest's first styling salon to opening the first U.S. salon in Russia.

Joe Francis was a visionary and a pioneer of franchising development. He was a colorful and enthusiastic leader who kept a promise to himself to persevere in spite of obstacles and "nay sayers." Behind the scenes, Joe recognized his most devoted employee, Florence, who for 30 years pitched stories to local media, directed newsletter publication, advanced the company through public relations and served on the Board of Directors—without ever receiving a paycheck.

The success of The Barbers is rooted in the philosophy of the Francis's commitment to bringing loyal employees along with them as their company grew. They helped their family of franchisees and employees become as successful as they could be, knowing they were the catalysts for the company's progress.

Joe also developed and launched a franchise concept, Inner Circle International, to mentor small-business owners and was instrumental in forming a degree program in franchising at the University of St. Thomas in Minneapolis. He sat on the board of directors of numerous organizations, most importantly, the International Franchise Association, in Washington, D.C., the American Institute for Entrepreneurs and The National Association of Cosmetologists. In 1993, IFA honored Joe with its Entrepreneur of the Year Award.

One of Joe's final wishes and Florence's continuing work is the promotion of Cosmetology careers. Through the non-profit Joe Francis Scholarship Foundation, deserving students will receive the financial support needed to attend cosmetology school. Florence's position on the IFA's Board of Directors and the scholarship foundation are examples of the Francis' commitment to strengthen the industry as a whole. As their actions have demonstrated, what matters most in any endeavor are the people who make it happen and their leaders.

*Contributions are appreciated and may be sent to: Joe Francis Scholarship Foundation—P.O. Box 50625, Minneapolis, MN 55405

CHAPTER 17

JOE FRANCIS AWARDS & RECOGNITION

1963 Award of Merit Winner—Worldwide Flat Top and Crew Cut Contest.

1963 2nd Place—World Flat Top Haircut Champion.

1965 Award of Excellence for performance as Emcee and Chairman of Men's Haircutting Contests.

1966 Upper Midwest Barber of the Year.

1966 Good Neighbor Award—WCCO Radio, Minneapolis, MN.

1968 Featured Guest Artist—Central & Western Canadian Barber Show.

1981 Entrepreneurial Certificate of Achievement—MN Business Hall of Fame.

1986 Venture Magazine-The Barbers ranked 6th fastest-growing franchise Co. in US.

1989 Joe Francis was voted onto the International Franchise Association Board of Directors.

1990 Minnesota Entrepreneur of the Year.

1990 United States Entrepreneur of the Year—Inc. Magazine.

1992 Lifetime Achievement Award—The Barbers Board of Directors.

1992 Master of the Craft Award—International Art and Fashion Group.

1992 Received International Franchise Association—Entrepreneur of the Year.

1993 City of St. Paul proclamation—"The Barbers" Day.

1994 Honored Member—Who's Who Registry of Global Business Leaders.

THE BARBERS AWARDS & RECOGNITION

1995 Success Magazine—Rated #12 in the top 100 US Franchises.

1996 Success Magazine—The Barbers is ranked 28th top franchise company in US and the only hair company in the top 100!

1996 Nat'l. Cosmetology Assn. of MN—Proclamation for 40 years of industry Leadership and Excellence.

1997 Franchise Gold Magazine—The Barbers is ranked #10 of all US franchise companies with 500-1,000 units.

1997 Franchise Times—The Barbers is ranked #11 of the top 200 US franchise companies and in sub-categories ranked #2 in ratings for health & Personal care and #2 for training and support to franchisees.

1998 Income Opportunities Magazine—The Barbers is ranked #2 of the top 25 US franchises for having the most satisfied franchisees.

1998 Success Magazine—The Barbers is ranked #28 of top franchises in U.S. And again, only Hair Company in the 100 listed.

1998 Nations Business Magazine—The Barbers is one of the seven franchise companies featured. Seen as a franchise organization with all the ingredients to become a legend, with concept, vision, talent, enthusiasm and ability...967 stores, 38% increase in earnings, building an average of 86 new salons per year for past five years.

1998 Corporate Report—Ranked #5 in return to shareholders, #9 in increased income, #9 in equity growth, #10 in increased revenues, #11 of 20 best growing companies in MN.

1998 Venture Magazine—Listed as one of 6 most successful businesses in MN.

1998 Forbes Magazine—Rated as one of the 200 best overall companies in the US based on the toughest screening in 20 years—considering factors such as growth in sales, return on equity, positive cash flow, 5 years of return on earnings of 20% or more.

1998 Success Magazine—Ranked as one of the top 100 Franchises companies in the U.S.

1999 Entrepreneur Magazine—Franchise 500 Edition listing the best franchises to start. Cost Cutters is rated # 2 in hair care.

1999 Working Women Magazine—Rated one of the top 500 women-owned businesses in the United States

1999 City Business Magazine—The Barbers is ranked #10 in largest franchise store revenues in Minnesota.

1999 International Franchise Association Hall of Fame Honor—Awarded to Joseph and Florence Francis... Franchise Hall of Fame, Washington, DC

In addition to all of the Company awards, a great number of the Stylists, Managers and Franchisees have also won competitive awards throughout the history of the company.